POCKET PORCHLIGHTS

Reflections, Insights and Recommendations *for*
Helping Young Adults Succeed in Business and Life

by

Scott Abbott

authorHOUSE®

AuthorHouse™
1663 Liberty Drive, Suite 200
Bloomington, IN 47403
www.authorhouse.com
Phone: 1-800-839-8640

First published by AuthorHouse 12/27/2007

ISBN: 978-1-4343-1812-1 (sc)
ISBN: 978-1-4343-1813-8 (hc)

For volume orders or education discounts, please visit: www.pocketporchlights.com.
To contact Scott Abbott, please email scott@pocketporchlights.com.

Printed in the United States of America
Bloomington, Indiana

This book is printed on acid-free paper.

This book is dedicated to ...

My parents, who first turned the porch lights on for me ...
My siblings, who grew up with me under those porch lights ...
My wife, who keeps the porch lights on for me now ...
My children, who give my porch lights purpose ...
And the rest of our family and friends, who are always
welcome to visit with us by the glow of our porch lights.

This book is also dedicated to you and your family.

BUT ... business is business! And business must grow
regardless of crummies in tummies, you know.

UNLESS someone like you cares a whole awful lot,
nothing is going to get better. It's not.

Dr. Seuss
The Lorax

TABLE OF CONTENTS

INTRODUCTION

My Purpose and Gratitude

"Take away the cause, and the effect ceases."

MIGUEL DE CERVANTES

reetings and salutations. On behalf of the many people who helped inspire this book, I hope that you and those you love are happy and doing well. If you're graduating, starting a new job, or just trying a new approach to life, then congratulations, and thank you.

I also want to thank all of the people who helped shape this book, and me, for that matter. Thanks to their support, and the influence (both good and bad) from thousands of others, I feel pretty confident that the following reflections, insights, and recommendations will complement your classroom knowledge, as well as your previous work/life experiences, and be an asset to your endeavors. Sound good?

Now, since you're the kind of person who likes these kinds of books, and therefore evidently, likes to improve yourself (you do, don't you?) — I'm going to assume that you already have some of the attributes that are essential to success in both business and life. Attributes like compassion, accountability, determination, aptitude, a sense of humor, and the wherewithal to juggle work, play, and relationships. Great stuff. Even better, by the time you're done with this book, I sincerely hope that you'll be more equipped to deal with the realities, and surrealities, that arise in everyday situations. More equipped is good.

Charlton Ogburn Jr., a prolific writer and the author of a dozen books, wrote that "being unready and ill-equipped is what you have to expect in life." He calls it our "universal predicament." Granted, we often go unprepared into our adventures, and it's a given that we can't know what we don't know. Be that as it may, we should always do our best to be honest and forthright about what we actually do know, as opposed to what we think we can figure out once we get there. After all, being unprepared is difficult enough as it is, especially if we can help it. But being busted as a phony is worse. Phonies are bad.

That's really what this is about: Getting you better prepared, more aware, and more confident; helping you avoid a few missteps and mistakes (not all, but some); becoming a better person and a better professional; and ultimately, being happy and more successful in business and life. That's the goal. Goals are good.

So, what do you think? Is a book like this worth the price of admission? Which in this case I guess, is really just the cost of the book, and the time spent reading it. More importantly, however, the value of the book is the benefit of learning new things, having a little fun in the process, and hopefully, after it's all read and done, being a better person for it. If this book was in a MasterCard commercial (can you say "daydreamer"), it might go something like this: Price of the book: $21.95. Time spent writing it: Over five years. Time spent reading it: About two and a half hours. Upside benefit of learning new stuff, and getting motivated to live a happier life: Priceless.

That's what you get out of the book. What do I get out of it? Well, in the spirit of total disclosure, I've written this for you and your family, because I consider it my heartfelt civic duty to help. But I also did it for myself (darn that ego), and my kids (who think it would be pretty cool for their dad to write a book), and for my family and friends, who say they'd like to see me put my experiences and observations into written words (I guess that means their tired of hearing me talk).

Honestly though, it's not about me. It's about you, and helping you be the best you can be. Really.

While we're on the disclosure track, it's important to declare that what's written in these pages stems from my activities and interpretations of many things. Who we are, what we think, and how we behave — are byproducts of all that we see, read, and experience. In other words, we get influenced by everything. The trick is in deciding which things to come into contact with, and how much to let those things influence who we are, what we think, and how we behave. You'd agree, no?

That said, I don't always remember who deserves credit, or everyone I should thank, or reprimand, for what I have to say. What's funny is, I've got a great memory — it's just too short. This could have something to do with what my wife thinks (and rightfully so) is a short and wavering attention span. But I do love her, and my kids ... and my parents and my brothers and sister ... and their families ... and my in-laws ... and my dog whose always happy to see me ... and I also like cookie dough ice cream, golf, blueberry pie, the Cubbies and the Indianapolis Colts ... but not like I love my family of course. I wonder what's for dinner? Oh yea, so the fact that I have a suspect memory, and a short and wavy attention span, requires me to thank everybody I've known, and everything that I've seen and read, for the help and inspiration.

I also want to thank my friends and colleagues, as well as my loving family for being, well, my loving family. And finally, I want to thank you, the reader, for your commitment to being better: mentally, emotionally, physically, and spiritually. Better is good.

I wish you all the best for a great career, and a fantastic life.

Hope you enjoy the book.

Scott

PS: I assume you like good music. After all, life and music just go together, like warm cookies and cold milk. That said, this book is heavily influenced by songs and their lyrics. Music also motivated me while writing (and rewriting) this book. So to enhance your overall reading experience, I encourage you to listen to the music you care most about while you read, and then after, when you can sing and dance if you like. Music's good.

POCKET
PORCHLIGHTS

ADMISSIONS AND APPRECIATIONS

Who We Are, and Why We Do What We Do

*"Knowing is not enough, we must apply.
Willing is not enough, we must do."*

JOHAN VON GOETHE

We've all heard people say, "If I only knew *then* what I know *now*..." The problem with this kind of yearning is that it's all about the past, not the future. And we can't change the past.

But what if we modify that concept and rearrange it to an achievable reality, like, "If I only knew *now* what I'll know *then*..." The phrase becomes hopeful, not wistful. It becomes meaningful and relevant. That's because we're leveraging other people's experiences and hindsight, which are passed on to us as insight. By extension, we get to use that insight, as our own foresight. Foresight's good.

Henry Ford, the founder of the Ford Motor Company, said that, before everything else, getting ready is the secret to success. Given Ford's recent financial and operational problems, it seems that he forgot to tell his successors that staying ready and fit are important, as well. Again, that's what this is about: Helping you get fit and ready; staying fit and ready, and accelerating your success. Cool?

Take the advice of a guy who learned a lot of stuff the hard way. You see, while I graduated from school with decent grades and lots of assumptions, I was still highly unprepared, and to my detriment, overconfident, nonetheless. Especially in terms of what

4

I thought I knew about business and people, and how my life, inside and outside of work, was going to change me, as well as those around me. Heck, I could write a book about what I didn't know about business and life. Anyway, what I lacked in readiness and preparation, I made up for in boldness. It was not a good strategy, and I was ultimately forced to (gulp) change. Turns out that change is difficult. Even good change.

While there may be something to learning "on the job," through the "school of hard knocks," or even "baptism by fire," it doesn't mean that we shouldn't look for help, do our homework, and be prepared. After all, a pat on the back for a job well done, is a heck of a lot better than the proverbial kick in the butt for a job done poorly. Reprimands are bad.

One of the biggest mistakes we make is assuming that we'll get off to a great start with our new jobs; become invaluable employees from the very first day; enjoy loads of fun and lots of happiness, and be substantially rewarded for our work.

Guess what? It's probably not going to happen, even if we're gutsy, or book-smart, talented, and school-trained to do specific jobs. In fact, it's dangerous to overestimate ourselves, thinking that we can show up and hit the ground running. It doesn't matter if you're the new intern or the new mayor: you're not going to completely know what you need to do, or what it's all about, until you do it, and then do it some more. Even common sense (or Spidey senses), won't help us out completely, because the fact is, common sense is not so common (and you're not Spider-Man). As Mark Twain said, "It ain't what you don't know that gets you into trouble. It's what you know that just ain't so." How true.

Or, take John Mayer, who sings so eloquently about the bitter/sweet "train of life." No, we can't stop it. And sure, the train will be bumpy and discouraging sometimes, and we'll have to travel with some unlikable passengers. But there will be more times when the ride is smooth and encouraging, with lots of likeable companions … especially if we have the right attitude, and the right support. Right's good.

This means that you can't just wait around for the world to change in your favor. (Sorry to disagree with you on that one Mr. Mayer. But I do like the song!) Frankly, waiting on the world to change is not realistic, and not all that smart. The fact is, your time is here, and you're time is now (with a nod to another J.M. — John Mellencamp). You're the future and the present, so get onboard and be a good passenger. Better yet, jump up in the front seat, buckle-up, and help drive. After all, nobody likes a backseat driver. Nobody.

Speaking of your likeable companions, this is probably a good time to give you some more information about myself. After all, it might help to get to know me a little better, so that you can feel more comfortable with me, and more confident about what I have to say. Mostly, I think it's important to admit what I know, and what I don't — which is an awful lot — and why I'm compelled to write this book.

So here goes:

For starters, let's just say that I've had a number of significant experiences in my life so far: great ones, good ones, bad ones, and sad ones — and that's all within my first forty years. Like everyone else in this world, I also have much more to learn and a lot of growing up to do (parents call that "maturing"). But that's all right, because the day we think we know it all, or stop having fun and lose our desire to improve and be better: physically, mentally, emotionally, and spiritually — well, that day just shouldn't happen to anyone. We don't just do that for our own sake, but on the behalf of all the people who love us, depend on us, or just have to deal with us. Life's more than a two-way street — it's a multi-lane highway, with lots of roundabouts, and a bunch of stop lights.

Here's an example: Recently, during a very busy time of my life, my doctor suggested that I should undergo some traumatic, heavy-duty surgery to fix a bad stomach problem. You see, if my condition was left untreated, it could have become cancerous somewhere down the road. Not good. Appreciating that there was much more life to live, and my family to love, support, and protect (not to mention my responsibilities to my business, colleagues, and clients), my wife and I decided for me to have the operation. To make a long story short, I had the procedure done. As expected, I experienced lots of pain, and I lost about twenty pounds. But I don't recommend starvation as a diet. Starvation's bad.

On the bright side, above and beyond the benefits of the treatment itself, the operation gave me and my family the not-often-enough opportunity to spend more time with my parents, who drove into town to be with us for the procedure. For what it's worth, you never outgrow how good it feels to be cared for by your parents. Loving parents are good, faults and all. Appreciate them if you can.

So, while the reason for having my folks stay with us wasn't much fun, the fact that they were here with us was terrific. Their support, along with the love and caring from my wife and kids, made the bad part not so bad, and everything turned out fine.

The point of sharing this story is to emphasize that improving ourselves isn't always easy, convenient, or fun. It's not. More important though, is the recognition that improving ourselves isn't just about us being better individuals; it's also about those who love us, need us, and depend on us. Visa-versa, it's about those that we love, need, and depend on. Think of that as our personal ecosystem.

Now back to the admissions.

From a business perspective, I've had failure and success. I've launched several companies, and one very cool restaurant. Thanks to one of those companies, I was nominated as a finalist for a regional Ernst & Young Entrepreneur of the Year Award, which I didn't win, but it was still a neat honor nonetheless. In addition to starting new businesses, I've also acquired, managed, and sold some companies as well (and sadly, that very cool restaurant).

While writing this book, I had the satisfaction of working for a very big corporation called Avnet — which is a global, seventeen-billion-dollar technology distributor. During my five-year tenure, the firm grew by approximately seven billion dollars in annual sales, and our stock shot-up by more than thirty bucks. That was intense growth in a short period, and the experience for me, especially coming from my entrepreneur, small company roots, was challenging and extremely educational. Thanks Avnet.

Complementing my direct, hands-on leadership experience, I've also worked indirectly with hundreds of organizations, both big and small, including P&G, Microsoft, IBM, GE, Eli Lilly, Oracle, HP, Aon, Belden, Harley Davidson, Sprint, and Apple. But before all of those corporate gigs, I worked as a busboy, a dishwasher, a bartender, a caddy, a waiter, a house-painter, and a cook. I also did stints in retail, a newsroom, a radio station, a warehouse, and theatre. Employment (and the paychecks) are good.

All told, I've had a lot of different jobs and seen a lot of different companies: From small, agile, boot-strapped, super-cool, play-foosball-in-the-office, hi-tech start-ups; to huge, inflexible, not-so-cool, don't-get-to-play-foosball, low-tech conglomerates.

Through the years, I've been inspired by leaders and tolerated fools; learning commendable attributes from admirable people, and suffering intolerable behavior from unbearable jerks. Jerks are bad.

Now, from a personal perspective, I've been lucky enough to have love in my life, as well as happiness and good health. But in years past, I've been miserable and dejected — just like most people, some of the time. I've been worth millions (on paper), and been totally flat broke. There was even a time when I was depressingly alone and afraid, painfully unemployed, and I had to sell most of my stuff just to eat. Bummed and broke is bad.

At last count, I've lived in four countries, eleven cities, and twenty-four different dwellings. To my parents' and wife's vexation, that doesn't include one night in jail, and the times that I've had to sleep on the floors, couches, porches, and patios of fine friends and considerate strangers.

Thankfully, after all of that — and for the record, I wouldn't change any of it (mostly) — I am now in my own opinion a relatively secure and reasonably adjusted man. I live in a nice town and in a loving home, with a remarkable wife, two great kids, an insatiable dog, a crazy cat, and a lazy frog. Even my neighbors are cool. (Heck, this is starting to sound like a Mellencamp song, albeit a boring one.) Truly, life's a blessing: bumps, scrapes, bruises, and all. Life is good.

To recap: I've seen some, done some, won some, and lost some. I've experienced the highs and lows of both victory and defeat. That said, I don't claim to know everything or be perfect in any way — faaarrr from it. Like everyone, I have much more to see, do, learn, love, and improve upon (trust me). And with hard work and God's good grace, I hope to be given the magnificent opportunity to do so.

To be clear: we can never know enough, or be good enough.

Now then, while I can't claim to be an expert in all facets of people, business, relationships, and life … I have witnessed enough good and bad behavior in all four to have opinions about what works, and what doesn't. Moreover, I'm constantly amazed, baffled, and bewildered by how many businesspeople — supposedly even well-educated, experienced, and successful ones — don't seem to get some of the basic and appropriate qualities, attributes, and appreciations that it takes to be good businesspeople. With a specific emphasis on the "good-people" part.

That's not the rule, mind you, but it's not uncommon.

That's why the world needs you and your peers to be good, in and outside of work, because you're the next generation of leaders. Eventually and inevitably, your generation will be in charge of our businesses, government, our environment, and the entire planet.

No pressure.

Above and beyond business and ruling the universe, you're also someone's children, grandchildren, and eventually, if you so choose, if you're not already, you will be someone's parents. That's when you'll understand my motivation and that of other parents.

You see, most parents want their children to be safe and happy; ready, willing, and able to handle all that life has to dish out. And life as we know it is a glorious and bountiful feast, even though it's messy at times, and requiring lots of napkins (and sometimes even a bib, and some big towels.)

Now unfortunately, while most parents want what's best, they may not always say it, show it, or act like it. One of the problems is that some parents over praise and over pacify (can you say "spoil"), which on the surface seems all nice and good, but overtime, can set the kids up for a tougher transition when they try to make it on their own. This type of coddling can lead to the Stuart Smalley factor (aka Al Franken from Saturday Night Live). Sure, you remember his famous self-affirmation, right? "Because I'm good enough, I'm smart enough, and doggonit, people like me." But in reality, none of it was really true, was it. He wasn't good enough, or smart enough, and no, I don't think most people liked him. And why, because he needed coddling, and my bet is, his parents had something to do with his situation. (Yea I know, it was just an SNL skit, and a funny one at that; but what the heck, I'm using it anyway to make an example, I think.)

Worse than coddling and good intentions gone awry, some moms and dads propagate the disappointing attitude that the band Korn rallies against in one of its songs when they wonder —

and justifiably so — why a parent would ever make their own child feel like a "nobody." Regrettably, that does happen too, and that's a shame.

The biggest shame and injustice, however, is that there are some bad parents, as well as some evil, predatory adults, who are abusive and downright criminal in their treatment of children. As shocking as those sins are to think about or comprehend, it does happen. All we can hope is that children who are physically and emotionally abused, can get out of that situation to find peace, and happiness. Personally, I believe the abused get extra credit in heaven. Conversely, I believe the inexcusable deviants that do the abusing get appropriately and disproportionately punished on this Earth, and after they leave it.

Thankfully however, abusive parents and nefarious adults are in the extreme minority. The majority of us, even the absent, neglectful, or incarcerated — love and appreciate our children. It's in our DNA. And I've been told you can't change DNA.

But as parents, we also know that we won't always be there to guide and protect you personally, especially at your age as a young adult. That's why you need to do what you need to do; be your own person, and make your own way. That's a lot of what being a responsible adult is about, assuming you choose to be one.

You do, don't you?

However, you should always know that even though you physically move out and leave home, we parents are here for you. Wherever your journey takes you, we'll leave the porch lights on, just as we did when you were younger, and we all cherished those lights (real or figurative) that protected our house from the bad guys, and helped guide and welcome you safely home. Guidance and safety are good.

Even if you didn't have porch lights as a kid, or if you don't have them now — you can surely understand their sentiment and symbolism. Intuitively, you can appreciate what this book, *Pocket PorchLights*, is all about. If we can't be with you in person as parents, and if you can't always be with us at home, you can carry a little bit of your home and family in your pocket, as a representation that we're together in spirit; that we care for each other; that we're here for each other, and that we love each other.

To sum up: Let's be honest with ourselves and each other; admit what we should admit, and appreciate what needs to be appreciated. Admissions and appreciations are good.

IT'S OVER AND IT'S JUST BEGUN

Keep Momentum, Drive Progress

"It's never too late, to be who you might have been."

GEORGE ELIOT

In 2001, after reluctantly resigning from the first company that I started on my own (I'll talk more about that experience later), I was asked to be the Entrepreneur in Residence at Indiana University. What an honor! The job was easy enough, as all I really had to do was spend a couple of days on IU's Bloomington campus, visit with faculty and students, and talk about business, entrepreneurship, and life. Some of my favorite subjects. Even better, that event sparked the idea to write this book. Inspiration's good.

Due to my own circumstances at the time, coupled with the fact that the country was experiencing some pain and frustration from the dot-com crash (this was before 9/11), and that the graduating students were dealing with their own set of issues and uncertainty specific to work and life after college — I focused my presentations and conversations on three topics: reality, change, and attitude — as that was not an easy time for any of us in regard to those aspects. Indeed, it was a time of uncertainty for all of us. But to paraphrase U2's song, "Zooropa," uncertainty can be a guiding light. That's a pretty cool perspective, don't you think?

Personally, I was coping with a paradox. On the one hand, I was sad to have left the company that I started, and especially bothered at the way that it had occurred, both real (what actually took place) and perceived (what the media and others thought happened). On the other hand, I was relieved to be out of a tough spot; excited about forging a new future, and making a fresh start. Fresh starts are good.

That said, it might help to give up a few details about that situation, especially because I think there's some things that you can learn from it. So here's what happened:

In 1996, I started an Internet consulting company out of my basement, with barely five hundred dollars in my checking account. I had no employees, no prospects, and no clients. I didn't even have my own computer. I had just passion, drive, and a vision that the Internet was going to change business as we knew it. For that matter, that it was going to change the world, and our lives. If I may, so it has.

Within months, by practically working eighteen-hour days, I had managed to win some profitable business. I generated enough money to hire a few good employees, and we excitedly moved out of my shabby basement, into a real office. Ironically enough, our new office was in the basement of another building; but it had windows, a kitchen, and was ten times the size, and way cooler and more comfortable.

From there, thanks to the hard work, great attitude, and steadfast dedication of many fine people — we continued to grow fast and steady for a couple more years. We hired more people, earned new clients, delivered real solutions, had fun, and generated millions of dollars in profitable revenue. Profitable revenue is good.

Business was booming, and I got married. We moved into a new house. We had our first child. Life was great. But candidly, I wanted more for the company. Right or wrong, I wanted to be bigger, better, and faster. For the record, it wasn't just about making more money, although that is always a big incentive. Truly, I wanted to have a great company that had it all: great people, great service, great clients, great values, a great balance sheet, and indeed, great fun.

One way to get there more quickly (as patience is not a virtue of mine or most businesses) was by bringing in venture capital. In other words, selling part of my company to investors, and then using that money to help grow the company, and then maybe, just maybe, going public. In theory, going public meant a big payday for the company, me, our employees, and the investors.

At least that was the plan.

So in 1999, in what my dad called a "dumb deal" (you should always listen to your parents, whether you agree with them or not), we raised about seven million dollars in venture capital. While this cost me controlling ownership of the company, it enabled us to hire lots of good people, and admittedly, a few bad. That reality always reminds me of something my brother is fond of saying: We're all perfect twice in our lives, when we're born and on our resumes. (Feel free to use that one, he won't mind.)

With the new money, we bought other companies who were similar to us and could complement our rapid growth. We leased new office space and expanded our presence in the U.S. and Mexico. We invested in expensive computer systems to help the company run better. We delivered more services, worked bigger projects, and had a boatload of clients. Our plate was full. We did all of this for what we thought would be a better future. And not just for the company's sake, but for our people, partners, clients, investors, and the communities that we worked and lived in.

At the same time, we burned through lots of cash. We took in more money from investors, and we borrowed from family and banks. We were growing our revenue, market share, clients, and headcount at a dizzying speed. But we weren't profitable; quite the opposite. For the record, that grow-super-fast-at-all-costs mentality was prevalent and even encouraged by Wall Street and investors alike. Just about everyone running Internet-related companies, were doing lots of the same things we were. In fact, we were (stupidly) following their lead. Even the most prudent and seasoned of businesspeople were getting caught up in obscene valuations, and irrational exuberance. When in Rome ... right? Believe it or not, private and public companies like ours were routinely being "valued" at about one million dollars per employee, regardless of profit. You may not know it, but that's a crazy high number. At our largest, we had over a hundred and twenty five employees. You do the math.

In time, however, what frustrated us was that, unlike a lot of the dot-com companies who never really made any money or had any real products, value or tenure (as the famed investor Warren Buffet said, even a turkey can fly in a tornado), we did. Yet we fell into the same trap and classification as them. When Wall Street finally woke up and realized that profits once again matter, and that many of those dot-com companies were not only ill-conceived, ill-funded, ill-timed, but also ill-relevant, we found ourselves in an ill-situation that required us quickly to put the *P*, which stands for profit, back into the P&L, which stands for the profit and loss statement, which is a standard way that companies keep score. Keeping score is good.

The fact was, we needed to get profitable again (like we were before), come hell or high water. At times, it felt like both. Our debt was dangerous. New money and credit were unattainable. We were on life support. This was not much fun, and certainly not the great company we had envisioned.

But on we went.

I'll fast-forward through a lot of pain, uncertainty, and hard work that kept us afloat. Admittedly, times were tough, but we managed to keep the doors open and get the firm to a point where it could be sold and salvaged on behalf of the investors, employees, and yea … my own ego and self-esteem. At least that was the objective.

Then one morning, I got a call that I'll never forget, from one of the venture-capital guys (remember, they had controlling ownership) telling me, in effect, that I needed to leave the office — right then and there — if I wanted to save the firm and the jobs of those I cared for. The VCs said that they had an interested buyer, but this buyer wanted me gone, because they thought that I was emotionally attached, and they needed proof that the firm could exist without me. So if I left at that very moment, they would make sure that we all got taken care of.

For the most part, that was that. I literally left the office, the company, and my first "baby" within minutes of that infamous call (but after swilling a few shots of Pepto-Bismol) and drove home.

What could we do? Stay and fight a losing battle? After all, we didn't have control of the company anymore. (Insert my dad's warning here.) The fact was, we had to acquiesce, and hope that the best worked out for the firm, and the valiant men and woman who deserved better, and had bills to pay and families to support.

It was not just about me.

As a footnote, the company was taken over (too) many months later by that buyer. There was some ugly and expensive legal wrangling during and after the fact, which triggered a lot of mixed feelings and interpretations all around. But jobs were saved; the company and its clients were leveraged; and I got a whole lot smarter. A lot of people did. Smarter is good.

Okay, end of detour. Now back to the original story.

So before arriving on campus, I prepared a short presentation titled, "It's Over, and It's Just Begun." By using this title and framework, I hoped to parallel my world with that of the students, and also to reflect on how this outlook was applicable to life in general. While the title, at first impression, might seem somewhat glum and pessimistic depending on your disposition of choice (like whether the clichéd cup is half-full or half-empty: me thinks both), the content, emphasis, and message were absolutely the opposite.

The objective was to inspire and motivate sensibly, but I also wanted to be candid, real-world, and conversational. Although I was a guest speaker and was tasked to give "lectures," I didn't want to lecture. Nobody likes lectures. We like conversations; being spoken with, not spoken to. And those aren't just semantics. There's a difference.

With that in mind, I wanted to talk with the students and have meaningful discourse that respected their intelligence and potential. I've always been a big fan and advocate of a quote from the author and playwright, Johann von Goethe, in which he wrote, "Treat people as if they were what they ought to be, and you help them to become what they are capable of being." You'd agree, no?

Happily, our conversations went extremely well. I was humbled by how many students actually liked what we had to talk about, and that they commented favorably on the theme and message, and felt that my words were applicable to them as they were preparing for their own transitions. And although I was only on campus for a few days, the overall experience was a huge inspiration at that juncture in my life, and throughout my life since. Motivation's good.

Since having those conversations with the students, the phrase "It's over, and it's just begun" has become both a creed and a mantra in my life. In fact (and you could put this under the category of "too much information"), I'd actually have that and maybe similar sentimentality tattooed on my body, if I wasn't afraid of needles and a reprimand from my parents. Yup, the thought of a parent's scorn can affect you, even when you're forty. (True, I am my own man, old enough to do what I want to do. Who knows, maybe I'll get that tattoo by the time you read this book? Look out!)

When you think about it, "It's over, and it's just begun" isn't just some lame, bumper-sticker catch-phrase for a one-time event like graduating from school, getting a new job, or having to start working for a living — although that certainly does apply.

The fact is, almost everything that we have to do and/or deal with has a beginning and an end. No duh, right? But really, most everything's cyclical. School starts, school ends. Jobs start, jobs end. Companies start, they end. Relationships start, and they can end. Most profoundly of all: life begins and life ends, at least the physical form as we know it. As the ubiquitous, all-encompassing sound-bite goes … "It is what it is."

But wait. Before you think I'm being fatalistic or cavalier, I want you to know that I really do appreciate the fact that some beginnings, and endings, are much more difficult than others, requiring special appreciation and mindfulness. The more we value (in context), that things begin and end, the more we need to enjoy the here and now. If we can successfully harness what we learn through life's beginnings, endings, and in-betweens … the better we can navigate and manage the new beginnings, endings, and in-betweens. Does that make sense?

By the way, fate and destiny have nothing to do with anything. They're an excuse disguised as rational. After all, Darth Vader was wrong: it wasn't Luke's destiny to go to the dark side. Was it?

Our destiny is what we make of it. As George Eliot said, "It's never too late to be who you might have been." Unless we just want to give up and disappoint ourselves, and those who need and love us every time something comes to an end; or unless we're afraid, for whatever reason, to take on new beginnings and blame it on fate or destiny —we have to understand what's at stake. We have to discern what we have or have not, and appreciate what we could win or lose, depending on our choices. Then we need to do what we need to do; get ready, and go. In other words, get to work. Work's good.

With every new challenge, we should be better, stronger, and wiser; appreciating that work takes work, and hard work takes hard work. As an added bonus, the reward for our hard work and determination will help us know so much more in many different ways: intellectually, physically, emotionally, and spiritually.

The experience we earn, good and bad, is never insignificant. It's invaluable. It's experience. As Ralph Waldo Emerson put it, "When a man is pushed, tormented, defeated, he has a chance to learn something; he has been put on his wits ... he has gained facts, learned his ignorance, is cured of the insanity of conceit, has got moderations and real skill." By the way and for the record, I have a good friend who is a psychologist and a feminist, and she encourages me to point out that we should all understand that when an author uses the words man, he, and his — that the message applies to woman as well. Being mindful of equal billing for woman, there's a similar quote thematically from Nancy Reagan, and of course, she used the word *woman* instead of *man*, when she said, "A woman is like a tea bag, you never know her strength until you drop her in hot water." The group Salt-N-Pepa propositioned it a little more hip in their song, "Ain't Nothin' But a She Thang," declaring, in effect, that girls can do anything. (I'm not exactly certain that my friend had these quotes in mind when she recommended this footnote. But she's cool.)

Indeed and undoubtedly, girls and woman *can* do anything. As long as they stay strong and determined, and keep away from bad guys. From my experience (and thanks to a lot of input from my female friends), the biggest reasons why woman can't do something, or for that matter, when they do something that they shouldn't, or when they don't do something that they should — is because of bad boys and bad men, who unfortunately have the gall and impudence to misbehave, mistreat, wrongfully influence, and worst of all, physically and emotionally abuse. That's appalling conduct that's morally incorrect, and depending on the cruelty, downright illegal.

Unquestionably, it should be our unified hope that all women can live life without any man's oppression. Likewise, it should be our unified hope that all men behave like good men should. And good men don't abuse women.

It's everyone's world. Equal and united.

Speaking of Reagan, I'll take another one of my story-time detours (but again, there's a point to it), and tell you one of my fondest memories, which was when I unintentionally met the late President Ronald Reagan on the way to a meeting in Los Angeles. He was retired at the time, but he still went to his office in Century City at the Fox Plaza building. (For you trivia buffs, that was the building used for the Bruce Willis movie, *Die Hard*. Yippee-ki-yay!) In any event, we both walked into an empty lobby at about the same time: insignificant me and the president, accompanied by bodyguards. As we approached each other and met at the elevator, he looked me in the eyes, and with the most friendly, warm, heartfelt smile, said, "Good morning, son. (I was twenty-six at the time.) How are you?" To which I stammered, "Good sir, how are you?" He thoughtfully replied, "Great. It's a beautiful day." With that, he smiled again and walked onto the elevator. Then two of his bodyguards walked between us, making it clear that I was not to take the same elevator as the Gipper. I didn't take it personally. After the president got on the elevator, he turned, looked me in the eyes again, and said with a happy wink and genuine ease, "Take care young man, and have a great day."

While that was such a quick moment in time, thirty seconds or so that happened over a decade ago, I still remember it vividly because his persona, his "aura" — radiated. It was palpable. Whether you (or your parents) voted for him or not, or whether you have an opinion about him one way or another, I promise you would have had the same impression at that moment as I did. Talk about lasting first impressions. And we will talk about the importance of first impressions, later in the book.

There's another bright side about your new life and going to work for a living. If you think about it, you (or someone), now goes from paying for school (in one way or another) to getting paid to learn. With that view in mind, it's like it is with so many of life's defining moments and how we deal with our triumphs, as well as our trials and our tribulations. It's about:

- Perspective (how we look at things)

- Attitude (how we feel about things)

- Aptitude (how we work at things)

- Mindfulness (how we think of things)

I call that PAAM. And good PAAM, is good.

Whether we choose to have the right PAAM or the wrong PAAM, is completely up to us. We're in charge. Now admittedly, there are going to be lots of people who will tell you, in effect, the same thing. Most people, especially your family and teachers, mean well, and tell you these things out of kindness and love. Be that as it may, it's still probably going to get a little old and annoying.

I also appreciate that you might look at some of these well-intentioned folks and think, "What do you know about it? It's easy for you to say, you're not me." That's true, we're not.

However, everyone on the planet, including your parents, deals with issues and difficulties. At one time or another, we're all challenged with having good PAAM. Thankfully, most of us are able to take charge, persevere, and pull ourselves up by the proverbial bootstraps. Perseverance is good.

I know it can be done, and I'm not any stronger than you. Really. I know this, because at age twenty-seven, at the absolute lowest point in my life, I was living in L.A. with no job and no money. My cash situation got so bad, that I sold most of my stuff just to get by, and for a period of time, I had to live in an unpaid apartment without electricity (which of course meant no lights, no TV, and no fridge; talk about adding insult to injury). That was a far cry from what I thought would have been my situation at that time, having moved from Indianapolis to live a more supposedly exciting life. Yeah … right.

You see, within months after moving to California and starting a new job, I got suddenly RIF-ed (meaning "reduction in force"), which is what some companies call it when they let people go to cut costs. In other words, I got the boot. Due to my lack of income, a mountain of debt, and a heavy dose of frustration, sadness, and disillusionment — my life sucked. Frankly, I got so downtrodden that I even contemplated the most selfish act of all, not to mention unbearably hurtful to those who love us: suicide.

Writing about those feelings now, knowing all of the magnificent things that are in my life today: especially my wife, who inspires me through her talent, love and encouragement; our wonderful children, who make me smile and feel blessed every day; and of course, my parents, brothers, sister, my extended family, and so many other important people — I'm dismayed that I ever had such tragic thoughts, and reckoned myself to be an irredeemable failure.

But I *was* broken: financially, emotionally, physically, and spiritually … and just too prideful, and dumb, to ask for help. Then one day, thankfully, about four weeks into this heavy funk, I was sitting in a grubby cantina, scarfing down the $3.99 all-you-can eat buffet (me and about twenty other down-and-out bums), and it struck me, an epiphany if you will: It was time to get going. It was time to pack my bags, and head back on home to my family in the Midwest. There would be no more wallowing in self-pity, no more anger, no more tears. It was time to reclaim life, take charge, and get going. Giddy-up!

So, while I moved to Los Angeles with a truckload of furniture, an abundance of youthful exuberance, and a heart full of misguided dreams ... I drove away with just two suitcases and a backpack of clothes, some pictures, and whatever else could fit in my fancy sports car (a painful and expensive reminder of better paydays), which of course, I could no longer afford, and would have been repossessed if they could have found me. Living on the run from creditors is a drag.

What I lacked in material possessions, I made up for in an invigorated attitude. I felt fine, and happy to go home. There was more good news: I had managed to hook up with a potential job back in Indianapolis, although it required me to drive across country in two days flat. But hey, if Speed Racer could do it, I could too: Go Go Go! (Yea, that expression is from the Speed Racer cartoon. You do know who Speed Racer is, right? And his awesome car the Mach 5, his brother Spritle and his pet monkey Chim Chim, Sparky the mechanic, his sister Trixie, grumpy old Pops, and of course, Speed's blind brother in-disguise, Racer X, who was way cooler than Speed, and, I'm not ashamed to admit it, was one of my childhood heroes, even if he was just a cartoon. But I digress.)

Anyhow, thanks to a friend who wired me some much needed cash somewhere in Colorado, and fueled by thoughts of being reunited with my family — I was able to make it to Indy on an empty stomach, and an empty tank.

But I made it. And I got the job. It was an okay job with okay pay, but it was a job, and it paid. It afforded me the opportunity to live in a small, dumpy hotel room with a bed that folded out of the wall, just like you see in the old black and white movies. I basically ate PB&Js, soup, mac and cheese, and cereal for two months straight. And thanks to a lot of hard work, the right PAAM, and a little luck (did you know that luck happens when preparation meets opportunity?), I was able to move into a small apartment with rented furniture. Long story short, I got settled and got back on track, and never really reminisced much about that challenging time, until this John-Boy Walton moment. (You do know about the 70s television show The Waltons, right? If not, ask your parents or grandparents, as I've already digressed once too often.)

So, I do appreciate the whole "It's over, and it's just begun" theme, as well as having the right PAAM. Been there. Done that. Lived it. And got the scars to prove it.

As far as you're concerned, when you meet the next crossroads in your life, consider this: Yes, it's over — in this case, maybe your time in school, and to certain degree, the comfort of childhood and being a kid. However, it's only just begun. An exciting and brilliant new life awaits you: the good, the bad, and everything in between. That, my friend, is awesome. Appreciate it. Treasure it. Embrace it. As the Dave Mathews song "Cry Freedom" implies, the future is no place for your better days. Indeed it's not.

Now on a serious note, I also appreciate that, sometimes, the pain that comes from depression, fear and loneliness can be excruciating and unbearable. Sadly, that type of suffering can and does lead to thoughts of suicide. Understanding that, if you ever hurt to the point of desperation, or if you know someone else who is desperate, please seek help: On behalf of today's you; on behalf of tomorrow's you; and on behalf of all of those that do, and will, love you, or that other person. Before anyone makes that final of all final decisions, reach out for help. Help is good.

A Chinese proverb says that a journey of a thousand miles begins with a single step. Closer to home here in Indiana, John Mellencamp sings two great songs: "Your Life Is Now," and "Walk Tall." Taken together, Mellencamp suggests that we need to be careful in what we assume, because there's a lot of stuff that can get us confused and disorientated. Also, he tells us that having an enthusiasm for living, along with compassion, love and forgiveness — will help us get through life's uncertainties and disappointments. Absolutely true.

So get stepping, my friend, and have a nice walk.

While you're at it:

Stay safe.

Keep learning.

Be compassionate.

Have fun.

Exercise.

Think.

Work.

Love.

Enjoy the journey.

And remember …

We'll leave the porch lights on.   (And you do the same.)

CHANGE IS DIFFICULT, EVEN GOOD CHANGE

Perspective, Attitude, Aptitude, and Mindfulness

"Don't cry because it's over,
smile because it happened, and will happen."

ANON

I t's been said by some that the only certainties in life are change, death, and taxes. Kind of a downer supposition, don't you think? In an effort to lighten that one up a little bit, let's have some fun and think of a few other supposed "certainties." A couple that come to my mind are the certainty that the Chicago Cubs won't win the World Series, that I'll never get a hole-in-one, and that pigs will never actually fly (who invented that silly expression, anyhow?). You know what though, unlike pigs growing wings, I do hold out hope for the Cubbies, and making a hole-in-one ... just like we in Indiana held out hope that the Colts would win the Super Bowl: and they did! Dreams can come true, especially if we work hard, stay focused, and keep the faith. Dreams, faith, and focus are good.

For the sake of argument, let's agree that change is inevitable and constant. As the legendary soul singer Sam Cooke sang, "A Change is Gonna Come." Around the same time, another famous man, John Kennedy, said, "Everything changes but change itself ... change is the law of life." He's right, of course. I'm also intrigued by the angle that Tracy Chapman takes in her emotively poetic song, "Change." In the song, she wonders that if we actually knew that we were going to die, would we in fact change?

Would you change? If so, why would you change? And how?

Our ability to promote, manage, and live with change (and the uncertainty that it comes with), is critical in our personal and professional lives. Somehow, and I don't mean to brag, but I'm pretty comfortable with both change and uncertainty. Maybe that has something to do with how I grew up. You see, by the time I was twenty-six, I lived in Fort Wayne, Chicago, San Francisco, Minneapolis, London, Paris, Madrid, and as you know by now, Indianapolis. And that doesn't include the hundreds of towns and cities that I've visited around the world.

While the States are great, my ten-plus years of living in Europe were enlightening and influential. Granted, we moved a lot when I was a kid, but the incredible experiences, good and bad, were tremendously formative. There were so many neat things about living overseas, that I could write a book about that too. The bad boiled down to a couple of crazy factors: terrorism, and the sporadic aggression (you could call it hatred) against Americans.

When I was growing up in Europe in the 70s and early 80s, we lived with the shock, anguish, and uncertainty of terrorism, as that was a time when separatist groups like the IRA, which at times terrorized England, and ETA, which at times terrorized Spain — sporadically bombed and killed on behalf of their "agendas." Between grade school and high school, we were threatened with numerous bomb scares, and we actually saw the pain and aftermath left by a bomb's destruction. To a less harsh degree, but still impactful, we also had our fair share of taunting, name-calling, and fistfights with the kids who didn't care for us Americans. It tended to be a love/hate relationship: either they accepted us, or they didn't. Some even tried to have fun with it, by wearing stupid T-shirts that said, "I'm not a tourist, I live here." (That was like trying to put out fire with gasoline.) Dealing with those dynamics, coupled with the fact that we moved about every three years, is probably how I learned to groove with change and uncertainty. And I didn't even know I was grooving.

Sometimes I think about this early acclimation to change, like how a child who grows up in a multilingual home learns to speak two languages without knowing it's hard to do. If you've ever known someone who's been raised that way, you'll appreciate that they have this awesome ability to speak two languages, and that this ability just sort of happened: no books, no lessons, no pressure, and no sweat. As kids, they just naturally acclimated and adapted. That's a lot of what dealing with change is all about. Acclimation and adaptation are good.

With that perspective in mind, there's a misconception that gnaws at me from time to time, so bear with me as I get this off my chest. You've heard of Darwin, right? He was all about evolution. The problem is, lots of folks have his theory of natural selection wrong. Darwin didn't propose that evolution was about survival of the strongest. He said survival was about adaptability. Those that are capable of adapting evolve. Those that are incapable become extinct. It's not about strength. It's fitness.

Unfortunately, I've known some businesspeople that have used Darwin's good name and that incorrect view to rationalize aggressive behavior, and strong-arm tactics in business and in the workplace. That's not cool. If you want to learn more about how good companies evolve, adapt, and grow — I recommend two books by bestselling author Geoffrey A. Moore. One is called, appropriately enough, *Dealing With Darwin*. The other is its groundbreaking predecessor, *Crossing The Chasm*. Both are excellent books. Books are good.

Now then, what's so difficult about change? For one thing, it can be hard and uncomfortable; whether it's good change, like getting hired — or bad change, like getting fired. Come to think of it, sometimes getting hired can be a bad change, and sometimes getting fired can be a good change. It happens.

Change produces uncertainty, which is often accompanied by its pals: confusion, disorientation, sadness, hostility, and the ever-popular "why-is-this-happening-to-me!" As history's shown, and our world is still proving today in many sad and violent ways, people and society don't generally like situations that make them uneasy. Change makes lots of people uneasy.

But what if we took a more proactive initiative to embrace change? What if we made it our friend and our ally? At the very least, make change make us better, not worse. Granted, that's easier said than done, but let's do it anyway. At least try. Why not?

If we think about it, feeling crummy and acting crummy, because something is changing and/or changed, is a drag — so let's not act crummy. It's draining and a waste of time and energy. Life's too short to be a mad and angry grump. Grumps are bad.

At the pleasure of sounding like Mr. Rogers (by the way, Fred Rogers was an exceptional man, who lived an incredible life), we should all be fans of some of the time-tested, motivational one-liners, like: "If life gives you lemons, make lemonade;" "No rain, no rainbow;" "You've got to break some eggs, to make an omelet;" and of course, we have to appreciate the wisdom from Chevy Chase, aka Ty Webb in the movie Caddyshack, in that, "A flute without holes, is not a flute; a donut without a hole, is a danish." Okay, I have to admit that I used that nonsensical quote because it's amusing, and it's from one of my all-time favorite flicks. I also did it to make sure that you're paying attention. If you are, good. As Bill Murray, aka Carl in Caddyshack would say, "So I got that goin' for me, which is nice."

The importance for us to have a positive, "do-it-anyway," "turn-the-other-cheek," "take-the-high-road," "flip-that-frown-upside-down" mentality is imperative. Not convinced? Here's what

Mother Teresa wrote in her brilliant piece of writing called "The Final Analysis":

> People are often unreasonable, illogical, and self-centered. Forgive them anyway. If you are kind, people may accuse you of selfish, ulterior motives. Be kind anyway. If you are successful, you will win some false friends and some true enemies. Succeed anyway. If you are honest and frank, people may cheat you. Be honest and frank anyway. What you spend years building, someone could destroy overnight. Build anyway. If you find serenity and happiness, they may be jealous. Be happy anyway. The good you do today, people will often forget tomorrow. Do good anyway. Give the world the best you have, and it may never be enough. Give the world the best you've got anyway.

Hits home, doesn't it?

Earlier, we talked about Perspective, Attitude, Aptitude, and Mindfulness (PAAM) as important elements that help us deal with change. There's a fun Dennis the Menace cartoon, where Dennis is forced to sit in a chair facing the corner, as he was required to when he did something bad. With his mom standing behind him, fuming with anger, Dennis says, "But we'll laugh about this when we're older." Cute, yes, but he had a point.

As a parent of two young kids, as well as in my professional work and for that matter, just going about life ... I often have to remind myself of this perspective when feeling crummy in a crummy situation — that, in the big scheme of things, I should just let it go. At the very least, I need to put it into proper perspective ... and chill. Chillin's good.

While we're using cartoons, remember back to Timon and Pumbaa from *The Lion King* (now don't be embarrassed, it's okay to admit that you still love the movie like you did as a kid), and their finger-snapping, toe-tapping little ditty, "Hakuna Matata," which means no worries, for the rest of your days; it's their problem free philosophy. Not bad advice, and I bet it got you singing, didn't it?

Perspective. Attitude. Aptitude. Mindfulness: PAAM. How we choose and manage our PAAM is up to us. We are the navigators and drivers of our own world. We're in control (for the most part).

But wait, there's more. More is good.

Pearl Buck, a wonderful American novelist, wrote, "Once the *what* is decided, the *how* always follows. We must not make the *how* an excuse for not facing and accepting the *what*." In business, as in life, it's not just how we deal with change, but also what we do with change that matters. It's about the tangibles and intangibles.

This brings us to the difference between accepting change, and creating change.

Good companies and the folks who work for them, from the president to the receptionist, should understand and appreciate their ability, and their responsibility, to affect change. However, change for the sake of just change, without good, identifiable reasons; and whenever possible, a measurable return on investment (ROI) … is bad business.

Changing and improving, are two different things.

In business, good reasons to change are because of issues related to: sales and profits, competition, product innovation or obsolescence, globalization, technology, shifting trends in socio-economic behavior, bad people and bad alignment, operational inefficiencies, and most of all, because of the constant, unwavering drive to do better and to do more; that is, to grow more, sell more, save more, produce more, be more, and make more — in particular, more sales and profits, while at the same time, having happy clients and happy employees. Happy clients and happy employees are good.

Bad reasons for a business to change are appeasing over-inflated egos, incorrect assumptions, mere speculation and wishful thinking, the selfish need to create "silos" and "fiefdoms," the introduction of dumb products or unwanted services, because someone wants to hide their skullduggery, or act like they're working when they're not, and silliest of all, just because someone reads it in a book. (Nothing wrong with a little self-deprecating humor ;)

To ensure that change is justified, and to alleviate the infamous FUD factor (which stands for fear, uncertainty, and doubt), there needs to be programs and processes to ensure that change is properly envisioned and that it is designed, implemented, managed, measured, and adjusted in a formal and aligned fashion. We call this "change management." It's a big deal, and something we should all be conversant and comfortable with, personally and professionally.

Speaking of change and the unanticipated, Sherlock Holmes and Dr. Watson go on a camping trip. They set up their tent and fall asleep. Hours later, Holmes wakes his friend and says. "Watson, look up at the sky and tell me what you see." Watson replies, "I see millions of stars." Holmes then says back, "What does that tell you?" Watson ponders and then professes, "Astronomically speaking, it tells me that there are millions of galaxies and potentially billions of planets. Astrologically, it tells me that Saturn is in Leo. Time-wise, it appears to be approximately a quarter past three. Theologically, it's evident our Lord is all-powerful and we are insignificant. Meteorologically, it seems we will have a beautiful day tomorrow." After a short pause he asks, "What does it tell you?" Sherlock Holmes is silent for a moment, then says, "Watson, you idiot, someone's stolen our tent."

Now that's an example of reactive, "what-now" change recognition. In business, it's much better to have proactive, "what's-next" change identification. Either way, reactive or proactive, that's what change management is all about: planning for, incorporating, and managing the expected and the unexpected.

There are many business books about change management. Two of the better ones are *The Heart of Change*, by Dan Cohen, and *The Toyota Way*, by Jeffrey Liker. There are also lots of tools to help with change management. One of the best is from the American Process and Quality Center (APQC). They have a simple chart that frames the elements of good change management.

According to APQC, effective change requires:

1) Vision

2) Skills

3) Incentives

4) Resources

5) Action Plan

If we have all of these elements and can be accountable for the ownership, activity, and the results of each — then we can effectively manage change; be comfortable with change, and hopefully, get a positive result from the change. On the other hand, if we're missing vision, we'll get confusion. If we're missing skills, we'll get anxiety. If we're missing incentives, we'll get gradual change. If we're missing resources, we'll get frustration. If we're missing an action plan, we'll get false starts.

Sound simple enough? Well, it's not.

To begin with, each one of those requirements has many variables, subsets, and derivatives. They can also be conflicting, especially when it comes to balancing our personal lives with our professional ones. Mix in the inevitable input, recommendations, and influence from family and friends, along with a smattering of issues around religion, ethics, and emotions — and we end up having to deal with a lot of stuff.

That's why our ability to discover change, promote change, accept change, manage change, and live with change is critical. To that end, it really helps to follow a framework like the APQC, which can programmatically direct and guide us in determining, managing, inspecting, and measuring ourselves. Like in business, if we can't inspect it, we can't measure it. If we can't measure it, then how do we know how well we're doing? Measuring is good.

To help get you started, let me share with you my own vision that's used to guide, inspect, and measure my life. I actually refer to it as my value-statement, as it includes more than just a vision, *per se*. I wrote this last version in early 2007, and depending on changes within my life, I'll update it accordingly. It goes:

> "I will strive to be a good, compassionate, and loving person — doing my very best to live a gracious, giving, and balanced life. I will respect and nurture my mind, body, and spirit — so that I can continuously appreciate, embrace, and accomplish my responsibilities as a trustworthy husband, father, son, brother, friend, colleague,

neighbor, and citizen. I will work hard and smart, and do what needs to be done to have a productive, enjoyable, and beneficial livelihood. I will provide for and protect my family, and those who depend on me. And with God's good grace, I will live a healthy, happy, loving, family-oriented life."

There you have it: my vision/value statement. But it's even more than that actually. I like to think of it as my cause, my calling, why I do what I do. Causes and callings are good.

Here's the deal: If you do your homework and prepare; have the right PAAM, and look at change and all that comes with it as building blocks, not stumbling blocks … and as advances, not setbacks … you'll hopefully enjoy a more productive, happy, and successful career. More importantly, you'll enjoy a more rewarding life.

Earlier, I quoted Johann Goethe, the German novelist, playwright, and philosopher. He also wrote an impactful little piece called the Nine Requisites for Contented Living, and they are:

1. Health enough to make work a pleasure

2. Wealth enough to support your needs

3. Strength enough to battle with difficulties and overcome them

4. Grace enough to confess your sins and forsake them

5. Patience enough to toil until good is accomplished

6. Charity enough to see some good in your neighbor

7. Love enough to be useful and helpful to others

8. Faith enough to make real the things of God

9. Hope enough to remove fears concerning the future

Goethe was a thinker and a legend, especially in his own mind. (That was a dig on the fact that Mr. G. had a very big ego.)

By the way, as you will inevitably change, and hopefully for the better, you should realize that those around you may not always be comfortable with your changes, even if those changes are good, but especially if they're bad.

A few years ago, one of our new employees, straight out of college, confided in me that he was having problems getting along with his roommate and girlfriend. It turned out that their respective priorities and expectations had changed. They had conflicting PAAM. He had big aspirations and was motivated to focus on his job and do it well, to work hard, to be a quick learner, and to excel — so that he could take his profession and life to the next level. He was truly passionate about business, and having a good career, along with the income, fun, and stability that it can generate. He even talked about buying a house, getting married, and starting a family. The roommate and girlfriend, however, wanted to party and stay out late. They were much less passionate about their jobs, professional goals, and future. Having such different philosophies, it inevitably got uncomfortable for all three. Our man eventually broke up with his girlfriend, moved into his own apartment, and is doing great.

So here's a heads-up: relationships can, and will, change as you change. But you know that already, don't you?

That said, don't sweat it if you can't be the person you want to be today, or next month, a year from now, or ever, for that matter. But keep trying, everyday.

Progress is an evolution, not a revolution.

And for the record, just because I write about it, doesn't mean that I have my act together. I'm still flawed, just ask around. I have work to do, just like you. But improve we can, and improve we will. As Edgar Allen Poe wrote, "I have great faith in fools.

My friends call it self-confidence." Another scholarly dude by the name of Oscar Wilde wrote, "Every saint has a past, and every sinner has a future."

Speaking for myself, that's a very good thing.

THERE'S NO SUCH THING AS ENTITLEMENT

Work Takes Work; We Need to Earn What We Get

"To be is to do."

Plato

L et's assume that you're a young adult, born somewhere between 1979 and 1994. Did you know that your generation is sometimes referred to by sociologists, the media, and employers as the "Me Generation," or "Generation Why," and most distressing of all, the "Entitlement Generation?" That's a pretty heavy word, *entitlement*. In this case, it's not exactly flattering. So how's that make you feel? My guess is, not too happy.

Right or wrong, your generation is often described and considered by (too) many as being ungrateful, impatient, coddled, dissatisfied, disinterested, immodest, and materialistic. You're being criticized for thinking that you're all entitled to everything that hard work and its rewards have to offer — here and now, without having to work for it. Sure, this is a generalization, but it's what "they're" saying.

Don't believe it? Well, take a look at how Oprah Winfrey described her frustration with today's entitlement generation. She recently donated lots of money to build schools in South Africa instead of the United States, rationalizing her reasons to the media, saying, "If you ask the kids [in the U.S.] what they want or need, they will say an iPod or some sneakers. In South Africa, they don't ask for money or toys. They ask for uniforms so they can go to school."

Ouch.

Talk about guilty by association. She doesn't even know you personally, yet her, and too many other folks, are disappointed with your entire generation. It's a shame when your cards are stacked against you, even before you get a chance to prove the critics wrong.

Now I actually think Oprah is an incredible woman. Clearly, she's very giving, charitable, and smart; but she really took a shot at our younger generation. That's why some people, me included, are sure that there is more on her agenda here. Maybe Dr. Phil's got her doing some reverse psychology to motivate us to step up and fix the attitudinal problems between our generations, or at least to help bridge the generational gap. Time will tell.

For what it's worth, there are a lot us, including Oprah, I'm sure — who are not giving up on you or your generation. There are actually millions and millions of people wanting to help you and your peers deal with and overcome some of the obstacles and challenges that you're facing. We call them family. But keep in mind that, as family, we can only do so much. At the end of the day, we're not going to do your job for you. We can only assume that nobody else will, either. Personal responsibility is good.

That's our way of saying that you shouldn't look for or expect preferential treatment. For the most part, you're on your own. At your age, only you can get yourself out of bed in the morning, and put yourself to bed at night. In between, only you can choose the right values, behavior and manners that you work with — you alone.

Clearly, there are factors that contribute to this entitlement dilemma. Now I'm not one of those goofs who think that today's popular culture is the root of all evil (just some of it), but I do believe that we need to be careful of what culture we consume; at the very least, how we consume it. Let's take certain television for instance. I'm particularly miffed and disappointed with programs like MTV's *My Super Sweet 16* and *The Real World* (a more appropriate title for both shows would be *Absurdsville)*, which encourage superficiality and entitlement, and are enormously effective in doing so.

I think they're a problem. But that's just me.

For the sake of time and sanity, let's not go there completely; suffice it to say that a lot of us believe that some of these raw, sensationalist shows that promote elitism, negativism, decadence, debauchery, and entitlement are setting-up a lot of decent young adults for potential trouble, and a harsher reality down the road. Harsh is bad.

Here's something Bill Gates, the founder of Microsoft and the world's richest man, said to a graduating class of Seattle high school students. Specifically, he spoke about how feel-good, politically-correct teaching was creating a generation of kids with a poor concept of reality. That fact, coupled with some indifferent and give-them-whatever-they-want parenting, as well as the kid's own selfish, unrealistic expectations — was setting them up for disappointment, frustration, and failure. He sees it daily.

According to Mr. Gates:

1) Life is not fair. Get used to it.

2) The world won't care about your self-esteem. The world will expect you to accomplish something BEFORE you feel good about yourself.

3) You will NOT all make forty thousand a year right out of high school. You won't be a vice president with a car phone until you earn both.

4) If you think your teacher is tough, wait 'til you get a boss. They don't have tenure.

5) Flipping burgers is not beneath your dignity. Your grandparents had a different word for burger flipping: they called it opportunity.

6) If you mess up, it's not your parents fault, so don't whine about your mistakes, learn from them.

7) Before you were born, your parents weren't as boring as they are now. They got that way from paying your bills, cleaning your clothes, and listening to you talk about how cool you are. So before you save the rain forest from the parasites of your parents' generation, try delousing the closet in your own room.

8) Your school may have done away with winners and losers, but life has not. In some schools, they have abolished failing grades, and they'll give you as many times as you want to get the answer. This doesn't bear the slightest resemblance to ANYTHING in real life.

9) Life is not divided into semesters. You don't get summers off, and very few employers are interested in helping you find yourself. Do that on your own time.

10) Television is not real life. In real life, people actually have to leave the coffee shop and go to jobs.

11) Be nice to nerds. Chances are, you'll work for one.

What do you think? Does the tag "Entitlement" resonate with you, or people you know? Ready to do something about it?

———————————————

If we could, we should get every young adult and their families, a copy of *The Art of Living: The Classical Manual on Virtue,*

Happiness and Effectiveness, by Sharon Lebell. My sister gave me this book a few years back, and it's one of the most brilliant books that I've ever read. *The Art of Living* is Lebell's interpretation of the Stoic philosopher, Epictetus. Although Epictetus lived in A.D. 55, his views are remarkably modern and inspirational. If you had just one little book that could easily fit in your backpack, or by the side of your bed, I would recommend that one. Trust me.

One of the greatest contributing factors to the rise of the entitlement mentality among young adults today is, I'm sad to say, parents. The conventional assumption is that many parents need to do a better job (when appropriate) of saying, "I love you, but no, you can't have everything you want, when you want it;" "No, you can't just slouch around, wear and say whatever you want, and expect us to just give you money;" "No, you can't act like a punk, or spoiled, or bossy, or get in trouble without consequences;" "And absolutely yes, I do love you, and that's why I say no. In other words: I say no, because I love you." At the same time, most parents can also do a better job of praising as appropriate, and helping to build humble self-confidence.

Again, this is another generalization about lackadaisical parenting. Regardless, many parents, including me, need to do a better job at saying no, and sticking to it; even if it means having to shake the proverbial family tree. It's astonishing how such a small, simple, straightforward, matter-of-fact, two letter word like *no*, can be so incredibly challenging, sensitive, and difficult.

No isn't always bad, and *yes* isn't always good.

Here's a quick break suggestion: put the book down, grab yourself a snack, and Google "Entitlement Generation". Go ahead.

Soooooo (insert awkward pause here), what do you think? Accurate? Off the mark? In the ballpark, but out in left field with a bag over its head? Regardless, I get the feeling that you probably want to tell all of us has-been, old-schoolers that we don't get it, and to get off your back. The problem and the reality is — you can't, and if you do, you shouldn't: because we're your parents, bosses, and colleagues.

For a lot of reasons, and I'm not saying that they're correct or justified, but you have to accept these generalizations, and work from there. Sure, you can be upset and say it's not fair because it's just not you. But only you (and maybe others who know you better) recognize that. And if you're looking for someone's opinion as to your specific situation, just be careful of asking those who truly love you, because sometimes, they just don't see what they don't want to see, or they accept you because they love, unconditionally. Love's blind, right?

Let's return to parents. Now then, while it's nice to love unconditionally, it's not great to parent unconditionally. Parents sometimes have to be subjective and objective. Parenting is a real job, and like all jobs, it can be uncomfortable, and it's not always fun. Sometimes we have to do things that we don't what to do, like if necessary, having to treat our own children under the same demands and expectations that employees face, re: proper time and attendance, and work habits. And we don't do this under the auspices of "tough love" — but for real love, and for our mutual lifelong benefit. Good parenting is good.

The generalization about being part of the "Entitlement Generation" is not going to change anytime soon. It is what it is. That said, a Buddhist's perspective would tell us that we should accept inappropriate stigmas and innuendo, and consider our challenges, obstacles, and even the difficult people and difficult situations that we inevitably encounter, as lessons from which to learn and improve ourselves. While I embrace that thinking for the most part … I am not a believer, fan or an advocate in Nietzsche's flawed and problematic axiom that says: What doesn't kill us, makes us stronger. Because more often than not, it doesn't make us stronger, it makes us weaker. Again sadly, too many parents and too many companies use that inappropriate thinking to rationalize aggressive treatment. Not good.

Speaking of pop culture and trying to look at things in a different manner, the other night on a run, I got to thinking about the Dixie Chicks song, "Not Ready to Make Nice." It's a powerful tune. I appreciate the passion, instrumentation, and vibe. If you listen to the lyrics and know the story behind the song, you can understand and hear why the lead singer, Natalie Maines, is so impassioned about its message.

After all, we should all support the right to free speech, and like her, be disheartened that, especially in the U.S., speaking your mind (assuming that you're not spewing racism, terrorism, hatred, or bigotry) can generate loathing and death threats. Undeniably, it's also a shame that a mother would ever teach her daughter to hate an innocent stranger. Worse yet, that someone would threaten to kill that stranger just for having a different opinion about another person.

(By the way, doesn't everyone, regardless if you're a Democrat, Republican, or Independent, detest war? Sure, there can be rational to be in war, such as fighting for the right reasons, especially defending ourselves from the bad guys and protecting those that need protecting. It doesn't change the fact that war is dreadful. War is sad. War is bad.)

If it was my song, I'd keep most of the lyrics, but I'd like to change the title to "Ready to Make Peace." The message remains the same, but the goal changes. Natalie espouses that thinking herself when she talks about wanting to forgive, but not necessarily forget. Forgiveness is good.

The forgiveness doctrine worked well for Gandhi, Martin Luther King Jr., Mother Theresa, and Jesus — not a bad group to emulate. So I ask myself, what would they do if misinterpreted, persecuted, or wronged? Would they stomp their feet, and shout injustice? Would they get angry, and look for a fight? Would they give up, and quit?

I can't help but think that they would put it in perspective, take the right stand, and accept the reality for what it is. And we should all do the same with our respective situations, as this is not exclusive to the "Entitlement Generation." This is inclusive of us all.

We can all be better: better friends, colleagues, bosses, politicians, accountants, CEOs, doctors, lawyers, waiters, pilots, stockbrokers, truckers, athletes, coaches, employees, lovers, brothers, sisters, sons, daughters, mothers, and fathers. You get the picture.

Maybe you're thinking how hard it is to take the high road, to turn the other cheek, and to forgive: especially at times when it seems like such a dog-eat-dog-world and that we're all wearing Milk Bone underwear (that's an oldie but goodie from Norm, in the TV show Cheers). Well, as sportsman and humanitarian Arthur Ashe said: "To achieve greatness, start where you are. Use what you have. Do what you can." So let's: use what we have, and do what we can.

Now's a good time to talk about the differences between realism and idealism.

To be a good realist, we need to be pragmatically idealistic. To be a good idealist, we need to be fundamentally realistic. It's like a hand-and-glove allegory, with the hands, representing realism and being the basis for the gloves, which represent idealism. Without hands, there is no need for gloves. Sure, we can have beautiful gloves, but by themselves, doing nothing, even with great intentions and hope of being used, are just empty gloves. Until placed on the hands, they're only dreamers with good intent, looking for a noble cause, their aspirations unfulfilled, until they can validate their ultimate purpose: warming hands. Inversely, when it's cold outside, and more often than not, the world is, metaphorically speaking, cold — the hands, for the most part, can go it alone. But why should they? That's what gloves are for: to keep us safe, warm, and comfy. Comfy is good.

As you can tell, I took some liberty with that one. Make no mistake though: my message is sincere and matter-of-fact. We need to know the differences and synergies between idealism and realism. At times they're aligned, and more often than not, they're not. That's why we embrace both, separate and united. As the Robert Frost saying goes, "Good fences make good neighbors."

This realism/idealism dilemma makes me think about the quotation from theologian Reinhold Niebuhr: "God, grant me the serenity to accept the things I cannot change, the courage to change the things I can, and the wisdom to know the difference."

Back to this whole entitlement thing: On the bright side, there are some positives that are attributed to your generation, like being innovative and creative; being much more technologically savvy and astute than any previous generation; and being respectful if respected. As this is a major theme of rap songs, it must be true.

Because you're generation is so wired (wirelessly) through the Internet and mobile devices, you're recognized as being more connected to family and friends than previous generations. Careful though: high-tech can't replace high-touch. The more we embrace technology, the more we need to make sure we don't lose our human touch, and the more we need to live life in the real world, in person. You feel me? You also need to be very careful that you don't mess up your future by posting inappropriate material on Blogs and social networking sites like MySpace, YouTube and Facebook.

While it might be fun and cool to have your own web page where you can rant, rave, and share explicit information — just keep in mind that employers can (better still, just assume that they will) check you out on these sites. Once you post your private life and personal information on the web, it's no longer private or personal. Again, this reality might not be fair or right, but that's the way it is today. So if you've posted content on the web that might mess up your prospects for getting hired, or encourage your employer to set you up to be fired — delete it, and stop doing it. Technology's good, and technology's bad.

Where does all of this commentary leave us? Well, here's where it leaves us … in summation … the cold hard truth … take it or leave it … fight it or make peace with it … rally with it … or just do with it what you will. The simple truth is, drum roll please:

There's no such thing as entitlement.

Sure it's just a word, and the word has several meanings. True enough, given appropriate justification, there are those in the world who are entitled to some entitlement, just not you right now. Nope. So unless you hit the lottery (unlikely), or you get the chance to live forever in MTV's *Real World*, complete with those beautiful, whiny, over-sexed, over-boozed, attention-seeking twentysomethings — you're going to have to make it, by earning it. But you know that already, right?

Hey, who doesn't want to live in a cool house, with cool toys, in one of the more happenin cities? Partying all the time, hanging-out in hot tubs, and sleeping in? Working in Betty Crocker, out-of-the-box, ready-bake jobs that don't really matter? Being pampered by film crews looking for "reality"? We may want it, even covet it … but it's not real. That's make-believe. That's nonsense. To borrow from the songstress Gwen Stefani: that's bananas, b-a-n-a-n-a-s.

While I believe in lending a help hand, and that parents should take wonderful care of their kids, both physically and emotionally — I think there's a wavy line between helping and hurting, especially when it's time for our kids to enter the fulltime workforce. For the sake of healthy dialogue and healthy debate, let's assume that you're "spoiled" (for the lack of a better word) from entitlement today, and that you get some stuff and preferential treatment that you haven't really worked for, or don't really deserve, especially at your age. Well, it's probably for wrong reasons, and inappropriate. Sooner or later, it'll backfire, and more often than not, it'll do more harm than good. So if you're getting by because of your family's wealth, connections, or misplaced love, here's a tip: just don't get too comfortable. Remember what we said earlier about change?

The fact is, if we want something, think we should have something, and believe we should be doing something that we're not — the adult thing to do is to make it happen.

We have to work for it: with our body, mind, heart, soul, and gritty determination.

We have to earn it through work, time, the right PAAM, and real accomplishments.

We have to stomach it, because that kind of effort can be painful, demeaning, frustrating, and not always fun.

As I hope you know by now … I'm not here to be a finger-wagging, foot-stomping blowhard … preaching from some pontificating bully pulpit. (What's a "bully pulpit" anyway?) And even though I don't know you personally, I do respect, appreciate, and admire you — as well as what you're doing, what you're going to do, and what you're going through. I honestly do.

The fact of the matter is, just like my parents and yours, I'm only trying to help you:

Learn more.

Get, keep, and excel at a decent job.

Enjoy healthy relationships.

Have a loving family.

Be happy.

And succeed.

Success is good.

WE'RE A PERPETUAL WORK IN PROGRESS

The Joy and Importance of Lifelong Learning

"Thoughts lead on to purposes; purposes go forth in action; actions form habits; habits decide character; and character fixes our destiny."

Tyron Edwards

I'll always remember one of the more intriguing questions that were asked by the students during my tenure as Entrepreneur in Residence at Indiana University. The question was, "How complete are you?" (I know … that's just, like, so Jerry Maguire.)

Now before you get the answer, keep in mind that I focused our conversations on reality, change, and attitude. You remember my whole "It's over, and it's just begun" mantra, don't you? Of course you'll also recall that my message was about the importance of being humble yet confident, calm yet aggressive, working hard and working smart, understanding that failure is an event not a sentence, and knowing that nothing ventured means nothing gained. Moreover, that we're all a perpetual work in progress, so we shouldn't sweat the fact that we don't know what we don't know, and that we aren't where or who we want to be. Friedrich Nietzsche (the "what-doesn't-kill-you" guy) said, "Those who would learn to fly one day must first stand and walk and run and climb and dance; one cannot fly into flying." Progress is good.

In any event, my answer was that I was 57.5 percent complete.

How'd I come up with that number? Well, I did the math. The way I figured it, I had already lived at least one-third of the average life expectancy (which for a man in the U.S. is around seventy five years, although I'm signed up for making it to ninety). I was also hoping to catch the students by surprise, especially those who were actually listening. Mostly, I really just wanted them to think. And they probably did think, specifically, they probably thought that it was a funky number, and shockingly low for a guy who's doubtlessly got a good ego and believes that he's smarter than the average bear. To that end, my goofy answer generated some quizzical looks, a smattering of buzz, and with a little playful give and take, we had a lot of fun with it. "Show me the money!" (Sorry, I couldn't help myself; just had to go there, given the whole Jerry Maguire thing.)

So if I was 57.5 percent at thirty-five, what am I at forty? After careful consideration and deliberation, I'm going with 67 percent. Maybe if I keep applying myself, I'll get to 90 by ninety. Hope so.

What about you? How complete are you? And don't do the mortality math, because as a young adult, the math's basically immaterial. That really shouldn't be a factor yet, at least not one you should needlessly worry about — at least I hope not. What I'm asking is this: How aware and honest are you with respect to who you are, versus what you want to become? Then there's another tough part: getting from here to there, because you just don't know what it is you want, what it is that you have to do, what it will take, how long it will take, or even if you'll get there. Buddha said, "What we think, we become." Maybe we should all think more intently about what we want to become, while realizing that we'll never actually get there, completely. We should all believe that we're a perpetual work in progress. Hopefully, we embrace that reality, using that as motivation to improve and get better. Self-improvement is good.

In a previous chapter, I talked about change and about leveraging the APQC framework for managing change. Here's a similar "stractical" approach, using the image of a house, porch lights and all, to help us think about our goals, progress, and perpetual self-improvement as they pertain to our aspirations for our mind, body, and spirit. (By the way, "stractical" is a perfectly acceptable hybridization of the words strategic and tactical. Maybe it'll catch on?)

Symbolically, we can use the image of a house to help establish, identify, improve, and measure us as individuals. But we should do more than just imagine this house, we should document it on paper so that we can chart and measure our progress with how we're managing ourselves, and our priorities. Taken out of context, this might seem a bit self-centered. At the very least, it might sound self-absorbed. This is not so. The fact is, we can't provide for our families and be good sons, daughters, parents, husbands, brothers, friends, neighbors, employees, or any of those things, without a sincere and genuine self-awareness. The more self-aware we are, the better we can serve and be others-oriented. Self-knowledge is the beginning of self-improvement.

Make no mistake, there's a very big difference between being self-aware and selfish. Abraham Lincoln said, "Always bear in mind that your own resolution to success is more important than any other thing." Do you believe Lincoln was selfish?

Back to our metaphorical crib: Picture the foundation of our house anchored by four walls that represent our mind, body, spirit, and values. On top of this foundation is the first floor, and it's basically one big room dedicated to family. The second floor has four more rooms assigned to work, finance, administration, and last, but not least, fun and leisure. Securely on top is the roof, which signifies our overarching responsibility to provide for, comfort and protect those who need our help. It's a modest house, but its home. Home's good.

So how do we determine our priorities, motivations, and rationale for our foundation of mind, body, spirit, and values?

To begin with, from a mind perspective, that's where everything starts, stops, or gets hung up. We can't be anyone or do anything, if we don't put our mind to it. As they say, mind-over-matter. So we need to feed our minds to their fullest, and one of the best ways to feed our minds is to read.

I implore you to read voraciously, with a committed purpose to really reading, not just to pass the time or go through the motions. Take the time to read, whether you're reading fact or fiction, magazines like *Ode, Fast Company, Business Week, Business 2.0*, and *Harvard Business Review*, along with newspapers, cereal boxes, pamphlets handed to us on the street corner, and writing on the bathroom wall. When we find it, we should read it, whether we agree with it, or not. In fact, that's one of the most important reasons to read everything: to challenge what we believe, as we assimilate an author's opinions, ideology, and philosophy.

If we only read what we're comfortable with today, or what we're told to read because "that's just the way we think, and that's just the way it is," then how can we ever hope to be sympathetic, or at least empathetic, to viewpoints other than our own. What if they're right, or just partially right? What if? We'll never know what we might need to know, or should know, if we don't try. That's called willful ignorance. Ignorance is ignorant, and stupid.

On the other hand, if we don't want to be ignorant, and instead, choose to learn, understand, and experience new things — the best and the cheapest way, other than being on the job or there in person, is by reading. Reading's good.

Another great way to feed our minds is to listen genuinely. This one's not always easy, because unlike reading, where it's only one person — the ability to listen in the give-and-take of a conversation requires much more work. Reading uses just the brain, eyes, and maybe the hands. (Okay, sometimes we move our lips while reading silently and it can be kind of embarrassing.

But it's not a crime.) Good listening requires a lot of energy and focus, unless we're just listening to the TV, radio, or movies. I'm talking about in-person listening, which needs the brain, the ears, the eyes, the mouth, and the body. It requires "presence," even when not personally present, like when we're on the phone. Often, listening can be uncomfortable, because good listeners listen first and foremost to whatever the speaker has to say, whether we like it or not. That's called active listening. Then we talk. In between listening and talking, we think. Concurrent to listening, talking, and thinking — we express interest through our presence, *vis-à-vis* our eyes, mouth, posture, and hands. That's body language. We use active listening and body language to show the speaker that we care, and that we are actually listening. Sometimes it's easier said than done. Good listening is hard.

Our ability to listen is either an attribute or a detriment. We can't overemphasis the importance of good listening, and being recognized as a good listener. There's an old adage about why God gave us two ears and one mouth, implying that we should listen twice as much as we talk. The fact is, being a poor listener is a hard label to overcome, just like it is with most labels. So be known as a good listener. More importantly, really be a good listener. Do it for you, and do it for others. Listening is good.

A third way to improve our minds is by trying new things, meeting new people, and seeing new places — as well as through writing, prayer, and meditation. (One of my favorite books on meditation is called *Zen Training,* by Katsuki Sekida. Check it out.) We also improve our minds by doing the daily stuff that we often take for granted, like spending quality time with family and friends, listening to music, playing sports, fixing something, working out, cooking, and yes, even the ho-hum things, like vacuuming and doing the dishes. You know, as a busy adult, I now understand and appreciate why my dad enjoyed washing the dishes. As a kid, it never made much sense to me. Every night when he was home, he would do the dishes, quietly and deliberately. Now, every night that I'm home, I do them as well. For one, this is because I am my father's son, and proud to be. Two, this is because it's a great time to think and reflect. Reflection is good.

Mentally, we should strive to do everything that we can to make our minds better, with the ultimate, never-ending pursuit for wisdom, virtue and peace-of-mind. Don't get me wrong — information, smarts, knowledge, know-how, skills, trades, common sense, and general competencies are important. While they're good as individual assets, they're even better when leveraged collectively, because that's when we can start to approach wisdom, virtue, and peace-of-mind. That should be our objective, our aspiration, our dream, and our nirvana.

From a body perspective, our goal should be fairly simple: we want to be healthy. Sure, being stronger, having a few more pounds of muscle and a few less pounds of fat is the ideal, and if that motivates you, have it. Use what you need to use to help you be healthy. Just don't go overboard and get narcissistic. Again, the objective is to be able to enjoy life, with all its splendors, and its trials and tribulations.

Therefore, we need bodies that work. That means controlling what we can control.

As you know, we can all choose to behave in ways that are healthy, unhealthy, or even destructive. No one can actually force us to gorge on fattening foods and become obese. (Although the way some parents feed their kids, it makes me wonder.) And no one can legally force us to smoke, take illegal drugs, drink and drive, practice unsafe sex, dive into the shallow end of the pool, and reenact the stupidity from the *Jackass* movies (don't forget why they call it "Jackass"). Granted, we can be inflicted by health issues that we cannot control. Cancer, depression, psychosis, degenerative diseases, sickness, and sudden, unexpected deaths do indeed happen. Sadly, they happen way too often.

That's why it's important to appreciate the gift of life and our bodies, and to treat both with reverence and love. So, let's control what we can. Stay fit, and don't sweat what we can't do. After all, we're the boss of our body (for the most part) — so be the boss, and be a great one. Healthy is good.

When I talk about the foundational elements of spirituality, I don't just mean being religious, and practicing the tenets and written doctrines of a core religion. We don't always have to see eye-to-eye with everything that our "inherited" religion says or does. We should be able to enjoy aspects, elements, and mindsets of all religions. No?

Spirituality is about having a higher aspect to life, above and beyond the physical world, and the here-and-now. While I personally believe in God and Jesus Christ, I also believe in additional spiritual guidance and motivation. And yes, I think that God and Jesus are good with that. In my opinion, religion isn't black and white, right or wrong, we're in or we're out, we have it or we don't. Our spirit is what we make of it, and what it makes of us — in our own definition (assuming that you are capable of making that call). Again, in my opinion, spirituality doesn't have to come in a one-size-fits-all, prescribed, prepackaged formula, or in just one book. I think it can be an amalgamation of many. At the end of the day, I think spirit is an intangible, yet ever-present aspect to our body and life that helps motivate, guide, comfort, and inspire us. Spirituality is good.

If you want to read a really provocative and compelling book that can help you better understand the religions of the world, including Christianity, Islam, Judaism, Buddhism, and Hinduism, please read *Religious Literacy; What Every American Needs to Know* —

And Doesn't, by Stephen Prothero. And, if you want to read another wonderful book that leverages, mixes and promotes spirituality from diverse religions, read *Awareness: The Perils and Opportunities of Reality,* by Anthony De Mello.

From a values perspective, I'm talking about more than just being ethical, as we all agree that we shouldn't lie, cheat, steal, perjure, act immorally, physically injure let alone kill another, or do anything that's actually illegal or against the law — at least not intentionally, or without a very good cause — like speeding and running a red light to get your pregnant wife to the hospital. (Yup, did that.) More than just for being ethical and obeying the laws, values pertain to how we treat people and behave. To that point, values are also about kindness, generosity, compassion, courtesy, respect, listening, being a good communicator, as well as those "nice" traits that help us be better people, and moreover, better people-people.

Maintaining our values is especially tough when we work in the all-too-often combative, hardcore, fast-paced, short-fused, just-get-the-job-done, polarizing corporate world — where trust can be hard, support convenient, and styles gruff and unfriendly. And for all the wrong reasons, there's sometimes a misguided attitude in some businesses that nice folks finish last.

Wrong.

Nice businesspeople, and for that matter, nice companies — can, and must, succeed. That said, the good news is that most companies want both nice and productive employees. They really do. But here's the deal: Because we're nice and gravitate toward having likable, people-friendly, team-oriented, and collaborative environments — that just means that we have to consistently work hard, perform, and execute. Moreover, we can't act like fools, tolerate fools, or accept a fool's errand. Don't be a pushover, and you won't get pushed over. Our niceness can't be taken advantage of. We do what we say, and we say what we'll do. Most of all, we meet or exceed expectations, and we consistently deliver tangible, proof-positive results, with quality and good PAAM.

I'll talk more about this later and provide recommendations that can help you succeed. For now, just keep in mind that you should be a nice person, and that nice people prefer to work, befriend, defend, and hang out with other nice people. And nice people don't emulate jerks, even if they're powerful jerks. They're still jerks who'll often say that nice people don't have what it takes, the "killer instinct," to get the job done. In reality, they don't have what it takes, because they're typically one-dimensional and afraid. More often than not, they're intimidated by nice people who get things done the nice way.

Jerks, and their fraternal order of brethren and cronies, including: bullies, snobs, sycophants, schmucks, tyrants, tormentors, and all other jerk-like labels, just plain stink. Sure, they can do their jobs, and more often than not, they get results. But at what cost? Would you choose to work for them if given a choice? I wonder if they would work for themselves. I also wonder if they even like themselves. I think not.

Can you guess the typical reason jerks give to justify their intimidating, strong-arm tactics, and aggressive, bully behavior? They blame it on other people. From their perspective, their "subordinates" (we should all dislike that word immensely, as it implies an arrogant, better-than-you, jerk pecking order) can only work hard when worked hard. Rubbish. Threats and intimidation are bad — period. If that's the reality in any company, then the senior leaders need to look into their hiring policies and the system of checks and balances that are supposed to ensure that they are bringing on the right people, for the right job. After all, certain jobs, by their very nature, responsibilities, and paycheck — can be tough and require tougher people who have the courage and fortitude to get the work done, without a lot of hand-holding and niceties.

They also need to look at that person and their management in general and conduct a thorough review to determine the scope and scale of the problem, hopefully before it's too late; before good people quit, or worse, become indifferent and turn into creeping meatballs (I'll explain that meaty metaphor later) ... just going through the motions to get a paycheck. Apathetic is bad.

Companies often use the word cancer, inappropriately so, to make a point about a specific problem. That said, jerk behavior and management by intimidation are cancerous. The real bummer is when the senior leaders themselves patronize, praise, promote, condone, or encourage jerk behavior just because that person's "smart" or "produces." That means that they're either quietly complicit, active proponents, or asleep at the wheel. This is all bad. By being indifferent to poor behavior, they're basically supporting it. Anything can be rationalized if you want it bad enough. With regard to rationalized bad behavior, I guess it's true what Upton Sinclair wrote: "It is difficult to get a man to understand something when his job depends on not understanding it." That happens way too often.

Heads-up: When you work in a company that treats you like an animal or a prisoner, it's a problem. And when there are no guards to watch over the guards, or worse yet, when the warden is the chief villain, you have to just grin and bear it, serve your time, hang in there, do your job and do it well, irrespective of the treatment, because you need the work, and it pays the bills that need paying. Just always remember that jerks, tyrants, and all of their rotten posse can occasionally disarm you with insincere friendship and artificial support. As the saying goes: Don't get duped by a wolf in sheep's clothing.

When I think about that last cliché, I'm reminded about the story of the scorpion and the bullfrog. It goes like this:

There's this nice bullfrog, working diligently on the shore. Along comes a scorpion and asks the fine frog if he could give him a ride across the pond to the other side. The frog, being no dummy, said, "But you are a scorpion. If I get too close to you, let alone give you a ride, you will surely sting me, and I will be dead." The scorpion smiled and pretentiously responded, "Indeed, my good fellow — that may be what some other scorpions would do, but not me. In fact, I'll be your buddy and your ally. Just think how great it would be to have a scorpion to protect you and keep you safe. You can trust me. I'll do you no harm." *Interesting*, thought the bullfrog. That was a pretty compelling proposition to have a scorpion in his little corner of the pond. So after a few minutes of deliberation, the frog agreed and told the scorpion to jump on his back and they went swimming across the pond. After getting them both safely to shore, the scorpion jumped off and immediately stung the frog. As the incredulous and gullible frog lay dying, he asked softly, "Why?" The scorpion replied without hesitation, "Because I'm a scorpion. It's my nature." Once a scorpion ….

Another "rule of thumb" is to stay in a job for at least two years. Many of us have had or still have bad jobs, bad bosses, or work for bad companies, simply because we all have to make a living. Regardless of the treatment, and assuming that you're not being emotionally abused or physically harmed, in which case, "Run Forrest Run!" — you just have to suck it up, and deal with it. But while you're dealing with it, fulfill your obligations with class and good PAAM. Take the opportunity to learn from what not to do and how not to act, so that when you do move on, you'll know better. In fact, that's how we do some of our best learning: by working for and with bad bosses and jerks; in other words, learning from what not to do. As Gump said himself, "That's all I gotta say 'bout that."

Gainful employments, and getting the experience and the paychecks, are the biggest and most important upsides. Keep in mind that, no matter how bad it is, it could always be worse. It doesn't matter what your job is or who you have to work for; it has to be easier than, for example, fighting in a war.

That's why we should all be disturbed when businesspeople, consultants, and authors use military jargon and war analogies to describe business. Business isn't war, and businesspeople aren't soldiers. War is war. Soldiers get hurt and die. Let's not dishonor the courageous service and heroism of our military men and woman by ever implying an association with what they do, and the immense sacrifices they and their families make, with what happens in business. That's wrong and disrespectful. Disrespectful is bad.

Speaking of (self) respect, you always have to hold your ground with regard to your own behavior. If you're ever in doubt or in a dilemma about acting inappropriately, try the newspaper-headline trick: Picture your actions (or inactions) as headlines on the front page of your town newspaper. Would your friends and family be proud of you, buy extra copies, and hang it on the fridge? Or would they be sad and disappointed, and throw it in the trash?

Here's another thing: Do us all a favor, and mind your manners. Manners matter.

It's both amazing and disappointing to see how many people, in all walks of life, who just can't seem to mind their manners. It's one of the first things that makes an impression, and we never get a second chance to make a first impression. Good first impressions are good.

With regard to manners, I'm not just talking about the fact that we shouldn't act like a jerk, a punk, a bully, or be spoiled, smug, arrogant, yell, demoralize, or belittle. Those are given assumptions. I'm talking about basic niceties, like:

- Looking people in the eyes with kindness and a smile.

- Proper greetings and salutations, like saying hello, thank you, may I, please, no-problem, bless-you, take care, have a nice day, goodbye, you're welcome, etc…

- Shaking hands with a good grip, and asking how the other person is doing, with feeling and sincerity. Taking the time to authentically care.

- Being respectful of age, experience, situation and authority.

- Genuinely listening and appreciating the other side.

- Opening and holding open the door for another, or offering up a seat for someone who needs it more.

- Having good table manners, etiquette and social decorum; being mindful of our conduct while we eat, drink, and socialize. FYI: "all-you-can-eat" buffets and "open" bars do not justify porking-out like a pig, drinking like a drunk, or saying whatever's on our mind, especially at company functions. Many careers have been messed up by indulgence.

- Dressing appropriately for the appropriate situation.

- Professional decorum, courtesy, and earned respect.

- Using intelligible grammar and enunciation.

- Being fair and unbiased, and playing nice together or even against each other. We can play nice and play to win.

- Not getting belligerent and lashing out with harsh explicatives, menacing facial expressions, and raised middle fingers over the little mistakes that we all, at one time or another, have made and likely will make again. To err is human, to forgive ... (That said, I do get agitated when someone hassles me for no good reason. It also bothers me when people are late; drive too close to my bumper, especially when we're driving relatively fast; don't use turn signals; talk loud during movies; and littering — tsk, tsk, tsk.)

- Respecting other people's time, possessions, and boundaries.

- Cleaning up after ourselves, or even after others who have the disregard not to clean up after themselves. For example, I'll even wipe down the seat and the sink in an airplane bathroom, even if the mess was there before me. You see, I just don't like to give the next person the impression that I created the mess and didn't have the courtesy to clean up. Admittedly, this is a bit extreme, and I don't like it. But I do it.

- And please feel free to add your own as you see fit ...

Make no mistake: we should all be huge fans of individualism, self-expression, and personal liberties. What a boring and glum world this would be without uniqueness, differentiation, and personal taste. Distinctiveness is great. Let's just not be fans of belligerent, showboating aggression, acting like an idiot, being juvenile, and wearing a bad attitude as a badge of honor. If you want to hang out with the wrong crowd, or if think it's hip to destroy things, be mean and condescending, hurt people, and talk a bunch of foul-mouthed smack ... that's your (bonehead) prerogative. But before you go singing that lame song, just think about the guy who sang it. Do you want to emulate him?

Two more things to keep in mind.

Number one: Perception is reality. As much as that may be unfair, unjust, and downright superficial — and I would agree with you for the most part — that's the way that it is, especially with the people who are older than you. Seriously though, tell me that you've never looked at or talked casually with a stranger, whose mere appearance spoke so loudly about whom you thought they were, that you couldn't hear the content of what they were actually saying. It happens ... a lot.

Here's one of my favorite perception-is-reality stories. Four guys were playing golf. One of the men was a real jerk. Nobody liked him. It just so happened that the jerk was being bothered by some nasty bugs buzzing around his head. The other three guys didn't have any problems with the bugs. They were bug-free. The guy with the flies asked if anyone had ever seen such nasty critters, to which one of the other golfers responded that they were called Circle flies; explaining that they got their name because they usually fly around the backside of horses, in circles, just like they were doing to him. After a few moments the jerk looked over and said, "Hey, are you calling me a horse's ass?" The guy responded, "I'm not calling you that. But you can't fool those flies."

The point is, if you act like a punk with punk attitude, people will think you're a punk with a punk attitude. If you look like a thug, people will think you're a thug. If you come off as a problem, thinking the world owes you a great job, great pay, and all of the benefits that come from hard work, but without really working — think again. It's tough enough being associated with your generation's generalizations, let alone promoting a bad perception by grandstanding or even hinting at an entitlement attitude.

If you want to look or act like someone that the company doesn't want you to look or act like, don't. If you have to be weird, and do weird things — be weird outside of the office, in your own private life. Just don't post your weird stuff on the Internet.

Number two: It's hard get past a bad reputation, especially having a reputation as a cheater, a liar, or being untrustworthy.

Whether the reputations are accurate or bogus, they're hard to get rid of and break away from. In life and in business, especially now for you starting a new job with a clean rap sheet, the last thing you want to do is start off on the wrong foot by cheating, lying, or even exaggerating. In fact, you want to do the opposite by under-selling, so that you can over-deliver. That's what's great about new jobs, and working with new people: they don't have to know about your past problems. We'll talk more about expectations later, as they are important in business, and for that matter, in life.

Please appreciate, respect and nurture your integrity, reputation and character. This is a lifetime commitment. I know it's not always easy to tell the truth and talk straight, and that sometimes we have to exaggerate or say "white lies," especially when it comes to hurting or helping people's feelings. Just use your good judgment. When in doubt, remember the newspaper headline trick.

The fact is, you can work a lifetime on being good with respect to integrity and trust, but with just one little slip-up, it can all come crashing down in an instant.

So mind yourself, and be careful.

As Buckaroo Banzai said in the movie *Buckaroo Banzai*: "Wherever you go, there you are."

You see, nobody wants to end up lonely, rejected, unwanted, and unloved, like Rexter, the talking dog. What's that? You never heard about Rexter? Well then, let's tell his tail:

There's this woman who goes looking in the paper for a dog. She's thinking about getting a Golden Retriever, maybe a Black Lab. But what does she find? She finds an ad for a talking dog. "A talking dog? No such thing!" she says to herself. But there it was: an ad for a talking dog, and to boot, it was a Golden Retriever, as well. This was like a real-life Dean Koontz novel. (If you haven't read Koontz's book *Watchers*, you must. It's crazy, big time fun.) In any event, she calls up the seller and makes an appointment to stop by later that morning. When she gets there, the seller greets her at the door, with a sullen, indifferent demeanor. "Hi, I'm here about the talking dog," says the woman. "You mean Rexter?" says the man. "Yeah, he's in the back, sitting on the couch. You can have him if you want. No charge."

Wow, that's strange, thinks the lady. *Why would this guy want to get rid of a talking dog, if indeed it was true?* So she walks on in, goes in the back, and there is this beautiful dog, sitting on the couch, watching TV. Perplexed, she just stands there for a moment, wondering how you start off a conversation with a talking dog.

After a few uncomfortable moments, she says, "Ummm, are you Rexter, and do you talk?" Sure enough, the dog quickly looks up from the TV, stares at her enthusiastically, and says, in an excited voice, "Yeah, that's me, Rexter." *Incredible*, she thinks. *Absolutely incredible.* She has to know more. "So what's your story, I mean, where, what, how did you get to be like this," she inquires.

"Well, it's a fascinating story," declares Rexter, eagerly. "You see, I was born in Eastern Romani, to a vagabond family of traveling magicians. Sensing that I had a special gift, they taught me to speak. Unfortunately, the empirical czar of East Romani, Ludwig Von Munchenson, learned of my gifts; captured me, and made me serve in his royal entourage. Fortunately, when he became unexpectedly blinded by his own misthrown boomerang, I made a run for it and jumped on board a cruise ship, as a castaway, headed to the United States. After we landed in New York, I finagled my way into Mathew Broderick's home, where he helped me learn English. For work, I became a bodyguard for Guiliani. That got me noticed and recruited by the FBI and placed on assignment for W1. Don't like to talk about it — but I took a bullet for him, earned a Purple Heart, retired, and moved here, to live quietly for the rest of my days."

When he was done with his amazing story, the woman stands there, motionless, absolutely amazed and visibly dumbfounded. She is truly perplexed, wondering why anyone would sell, let alone get rid of for free, a talking dog — and one with that incredible experience.

She goes up to the man and asks, point blank, "Why would you get rid of such an astonishing animal?" He rolls his eyes and says, "'Cause he's a liar."

Even if you're a talking dog, but you lie like a rug, people don't want to hang out with you. Value your integrity. Integrity's good.

Lastly, from a family perspective, that's oh-so-important.

Family should inspire all of us to be the best that we can be. Of course, everyone's circumstances with respect to family are different. Regardless, our immediate family, along with our extended family and those that we practice familial values with, are important factors for doing what we do, as well as why we do it, and how we do it.

Granted, I don't know your specific family situation. It could be great or a real drag. Your parents could be together or divorced. You could be married, dating, or single, and be happy with it or not. Regardless of your situation — and surely you have stuff going on and complications to deal with — do yourself a favor and call home.

Call a member of your immediate or extended family and tell them that you love them, even if it's out of your character or theirs, or even if it's embarrassing and uncomfortable. Do it anyway. Better still, if you live at home with your parents, or are married or in a happy relationship, do the same thing, but give them an earnest, heartfelt hug as well. Go ahead: do it. Hugs are good (and free).

You know, all this thinking gives me an idea.

Earlier, I mentioned a few TV programs that bother me. Admittedly, I picked on some surreal "reality" shows more than others — and make no mistake, Jerry Springer and his like deserve grief as well. But here's a thought: Maybe there is a way for some of the appalling TV to make up for its imbalance between bad influence and good influence. What if MTV, or any station for that matter, aired a positive, "edu-taining" talk show devoted to intelligent discussions about what young adults like you are dealing with? The program could follow a conversational, laid-back, guest-oriented format like Donnie Deutch's program, on CNBC, *The Big Idea*. It's a great show; watch it if you can. Our program would be unique, because it would be mindful of, and dedicated to, young adults. Our show would be structured around a formula for each day of the week, starting with the fact that we'd have live music and different bands every day!

In addition to great music ... on Mondays, the show could be about business and business-related issues. Then on Tuesdays, the subject might be dedicated to the mind, and we could talk about books and such that help make us smarter, better, wiser, and more aware. On Wednesdays, we'd focus on the body: staying fit, eating healthy, and developing and maintaining a body built for life. On Thursdays, we'll get into the spirit and values: through courteous and objective deliberation, we'll talk about ways and perspectives that can help bring enlightenment, spirituality, peace of mind, and values-based living. On Fridays, just in time for the weekend, we would focus on family and recreation. We'll discuss everything about dealing with the dynamics of today's family; but we'll also talk about lots of other things such as sports, sex, dating, style, vacations, music, food, cooking, and recreational activities that young adults want to talk about to help improve their lives and their taste. Taste is good.

I'm not exactly sure how many people in the United States make up the young-adult bracket, but it's got to be tens of millions, at least. Your spending power and influence are enormous. More importantly, you are the future leaders of our country, and we need all of you to be the best that that you can be, and that means taking the time to learn and listen; working hard and smart; being realistic and aware, open-minded and mindful, confident and humble, desirous and content; and all in all, being balanced. Balance is good.

By the way, the show doesn't even need to be on TV. That's really not the point. The point is the show's "purpose," that is, a focused and programmatic commitment to well-rounded self-improvement. Commit yourself here and now, to taking the initiative to develop yourself thoroughly. If you're going to take the time to get stronger, than take the time to improve your whole body — inside and out.

Speaking of well-rounded, I'm an admirer of Senator Barack Obama's book, *The Audacity of Hope*. Naturally, he provides some great insights and perspectives into politics, but he also does a great job in explaining the ideological differences between Democrats and Republicans, and rationalizing his reasoning for choosing his party affiliation. He also does an extraordinary job in the proposition, encouragement, and validation of our collective responsibilities. I'll give you a hint: they have a lot to do with hope. Now I'm not necessarily advocating Senator Obama for president, because the book alone didn't give me enough to do that; and to his credit, he set that expectation in his book. I just found him to be a good writer, and thinker. For those reasons alone, I highly recommend his book.

In closing, here's a brilliant poem by Henry Van Dyke called, *Be Glad of Life*. This poem captures the essence of life: why we live, what we live for, why we must all continue to pursue lifelong learning, as well as embracing the fact that we are all imperfect, and therefore, a perpetual work in progress. Van Dyke writes:

> "To be glad of life, because it gives you the chance to love and to work and to play and to look up at the stars; to be satisfied with your possessions, but not contented with yourself until you have made the best of them; to despise nothing in the world except falsehood and meanness, and to fear nothing except cowardice; to be governed by your admirations rather than by your disgusts; to covet nothing that is your neighbors, except his kindness of heart and gentleness of manners; to think seldom of your enemies, often of your friends, and everyday of Christ (sorry to interrupt, but please feel free to choose your own spiritual leaders); and to spend as much time as you can with body and spirit, in God's out-of-doors. These are little guideposts on the footpaths to peace."

To me, this is a perfect porch light poem.

I encourage you to find your own perfect porch light poem and clip it on your refrigerator — next to pictures of your family and friends.

Family and friends are good. Cherish them.

BUSINESS IS BUSINESS

Economics Wins

Know Your Company

Set the Right Expectations

Good Leaders Use Good Leadership

People, Product, Process, Planning, and Profit

*"Striving for success without hard work,
is like trying to harvest where you haven't planted."*

David Bly

L et's assume that you already have a job, or in the process of getting one, either now, or someday. Let's also assume you that have some knowledge and training that will help you within your chosen field. Remember, it's okay if you don't know much beyond your stated responsibilities, and what you were specifically hired to do. You're young. You're new. You're starting to work for a company that you've never worked for before, let alone know much about. And unless you've lied about your background, then your company will more likely than not be mindful of the fact that you are, in a word, inexperienced. No worries: after all, they knew that when they hired you. Right?

Now then, this isn't the book to get into the details about how to perform individual work or job functions. Also, I'm not going to get into the particulars on how companies and/or industries specifically operate. You can find that information on the Internet and in an abundance of other books. No, what I have in mind is to talk about business from a broad-strokes perspective.

I'm going to focus on the essential and fundamental elements that every person — and every company — needs to appreciate and be mindful of. And I'm not just talking about working for small to large corporations, but also not-for-profits and home-based businesses that have many of the same requirements. I'd even suggest, to a certain extent, that these elements are applicable in how we live our lives.

So here we go: the rudimentary expectations for any good organization with regard to strategy, economics, operations, people, management, and leadership, plus a few other things that we should know about. Reader beware: we're going to jump knee-deep into a mess of jargon, acronyms, and other business stuff. But it'll be fun.

To start, let's establish the core objectives for any organization, regardless of their size, state, product, or service. Let's do so by using a personalized letter from the Chief Executive Officer (CEO), and let's call the company, YourCo. So, the CEO of YourCo is writing you a letter to welcome you onboard; she's setting the stage for what she thinks about, and hopes that you'll think about as well.

Dear [Insert Your Name Here],

Hello and welcome aboard. I hope that you and your family are doing well. The fact that you are here at YourCo confirms that you're a very capable, talented, and friendly person. After all, we only hire the best. With that in mind, I'm writing to express my gratitude and enthusiasm for you joining our organization. My only regret is that I am unable to meet with you immediately in person. Over time, however, we will have the opportunity to get better acquainted.

In the meantime, allow me to share some thoughts on our collective responsibilities and mutual commitments. To begin with, there are two priorities to always be mindful of:

1) *Keep Momentum: Continue to leverage, promote, and enhance the good work that we are doing today to deliver on our value proposition and our commitments, in order to generate customer satisfaction and profitable revenue for our company.*

2) *Drive Progress: We will continuously enhance our company with new strategies, products, services, resources, operational effectiveness, and the support necessary to meet or exceed our objectives for long-term growth and profitable revenue.*

We are a high-performance, hard-working, values-based organization. We know how to innovate, acclimate, and make progress quickly, thanks to our collective experience, energy, and aptitude. We believe in superior teamwork and alignment. Although we manage by real and measurable numbers, using standardized processes — we're also adept with change and uncertainty.

With our collective knowledge, coupled with a friendly, "roll-up-our-shirt-sleeves" style, we're committed to effective execution through collaboration, accountability, and trust.

We're recognized for our integrity and good governance with:

- *Balance Sheet and P&L management*

- *Operational excellence, efficiency and productivity*

- *Delivering a valued suite of products and services*

- *Managing risks and controlling costs*

- *Responsibly growing revenue and profits — with honesty*

- *And we do all of this with speed, fun, great customer service, quality, and a team-oriented, people-friendly, can-do attitude*

Our philosophy is candid and straightforward: Practice positive pragmatism. Be ethical. Communicate effectively. Meet or exceed realistic expectations. Enjoy our work. Drive sustainable growth. And deliver profitable revenue.

Once again, welcome aboard. Thanks for being here.

I wish you the best for a super career and a great life.

Sincerely.

CEO
YourCo

PS: Please enjoy the enclosed book, Pocket PorchLights.

While the letter is a decent introduction to the overall business, and generic enough that it can apply to most any types of organizations, it certainly doesn't do complete justice to the underlying principles, realities, and requirements with respect to many of the areas and expectations that the CEO wrote about. So let's go a little deeper.

For starters, are you prepared and ready for the #1 truth of business? By this, I mean the raw, unadulterated, butt-naked, matter-of-fact, in-your-face, clear-cut, unemotional, don't-hold-back, give-it-to-me-straight, tell-it-like-it-is, with Jack Nicholson from the movie A Few Good Men shouting "you-can't-handle-the-truth" kind of truth? Here it is:

Companies are in business to generate profitable revenue.

Don't get this wrong: profitable revenue at the expense of corporate responsibility is inexcusable. My apologies (not) to the Gordon Geckos of the world (he's the rascally sleaze from the movie *Wall Street*, whose only good line was, "Greed is good"), but greed is not good. Corrupt, monetary greed is what gives the word "corporate" a bum rap. You see, companies in-and-of themselves aren't corrupt — people are. Companies don't lie, cheat, and cook the books — people do. Companies don't mess-up the environment — people do. Companies don't fail people — people fail companies. And most of all, companies don't succeed *per se* — good people drive a company's success. Companies are nothing or they're something because of people. Even a great strategy, or a phenomenal product (and buckets of cash), can't make it happen without people. The fact is, a company's most important assets, and conversely, its biggest liabilities, are people. People are good, if they're good.

Net/net: In business, the bottom line is the bottom line.

But let's assume that you don't fully understand the "bottom-line" expression, and that you only have a smattering of knowledge about corporate finance. No worries, because I'm going to give you a brief overview of some essential economics that everyone should know. By the way, I never took any classes in economics or finance. In college, I was a Communications major, with a minor in English. (Yeah, you couldn't tell by the writing, could you?) In hindsight, that was a big problem with my Liberal Arts focus, and I hope that in most colleges today those shortcomings have been corrected. More truth be told, even though I've spent my entire career in information technology, I never took any classes in that, either. It's pitiful to think that I graduated from college assuming that a P&L could have been akin to a BLT, that a byte would have been something bigger than a nibble, and that EBITDA (which is a fancy acronym that stands for "Earnings Before Interest, Tax, Depreciation, and Amortization,") could have been that band from Sweden. Come to think of it, that was ABBA.

Let's talk numbers, because we like them. We like them a lot.

Everything in business needs to be explained, measured, and justified through math. If we can't do the rigorous financial analysis, measure, and show proof-positive or expected results, using real numbers that establish and prove revenue and profit, then we don't do the business unless we're willing to take risks. At the very least, we have to modify our thinking. If we can't do the detailed math to rationalize new investments, new products, new strategies, new employees, or new equipment — then we don't. We save our money. Unexplainable spending is bad. Saving money is good.

Companies cannot be started, managed, or grown on just theory and speculation. They can't be built on just good intentions, well-written strategy, or eloquent business plans. Don't care if you're a tiny, home-based business — or a small, midsized, or a *Fortune 1000* corporation — you've got to do the (real) math, and love the details. At the same time, we need to be careful as numbers don't always tell the whole story. While numbers shouldn't lie, in-and-of themselves, they're not always accurate and don't always tell the truth. It's been said that 62 percent of all stats are worthless, and 20 percent suspect.

Numbers aren't always black or white, and they don't always fit neatly into rows, columns, and spreadsheets. They may need in-depth explanations because they can be interpreted in many different ways, depending on the view, expertise, and background of the reporter and the interpreter. It can be kind of like that famous George Gershwin song that emphasizes the different pronunciation of the letter *A* in the words tomato and potato: "You say tom**a**to, and I say tom**a**to. You say pot**a**to, and I say pot**a**to: pot**a**to … pot**a**to … tom**a**to … tom**a**to … let's call the whole thing off." (In case you're curious, that song is definitely not on my iPod, as far as you know.)

Numbers can also be a bunch of phooey, full of deceit. We saw this wrongdoing exemplified when WorldCom, Enron, and a few others screwed up in such a large fashion. Can you say "jail time?" In fact, the federal government responded to their malfeasance by instituting the Sarbanes-Oxley law, or SOX. Now I don't want to get too granular, because SOX is detailed and complicated — but it's a government-required examination that's used to ensure that publicly traded companies, above a certain size from a revenue perspective, are honest and accountable with regard to their financials and how the companies are governed. In effect, it's a mind-numbing, arduous system of checks and balances to ensure that publicly traded companies, in which many hard working Americans have stock and retirement money invested, behave properly, and are not run by greedy, arrogant scoundrels who give "corporate" a bad name.

Here's a suggestion: before we get into the following details, you might want to grab yourself a fully-caffeinated coffee or a nice, cool drink. This just might get somewhat dry, like eating store-bought stuffing, without water, on an August day, sitting in the sun, wearing a sweater, listening to bad music. Nah. You'll enjoy it. You'll see!

This man takes a balloon ride at a local country fair. A fierce wind suddenly kicks up, causing the balloon to violently leave the fair and carry the man into the countryside. He has no idea where he is, so he goes closer to the ground and asks a pedestrian, "Excuse me, sir, can you tell me where I am?" Eyeing the man in the balloon, the pedestrian says: "You are in the countryside, in a distressed, red balloon, exactly twelve feet, ten inches above ground, and losing altitude." The balloon's unhappy flyer looked down annoyingly and replies, "You must be an accountant." After a pause, the pedestrian says, "That's right. How could you possibly know that?" The balloonist says, "Because your answer is technically correct, but absolutely useless. The fact is, I'm still lost and you didn't help." With some hesitation, the accountant rebuts, "I see, and you must be in sales." The balloon guy exclaims, "That's right! How'd you know?" In a typical, expressionless, accountant-type manner, he replies, "Because you have such a good view from where you are, and yet you don't know where you are, and you don't know where you are going. The fact is, you are in the exact same position you were in before we met, but now your problem is somehow my fault!"

While this may be a silly joke (with a questionable laugh factor), there is usually a degree of finger-pointing, and "I-know-you-are-but-what-am-I" type of teasing between finance folks and the people in sales. More often than not, it's all light-hearted and in good fun.

Okay then, let's get cooking. Come to think of it, that's never a good expression to use when talking finance, as "cooking the books" is a bad thing. Speaking of the books, most companies use what are referred to as financial statements (the books) to establish, measure, and prove the overall health of the company.

There are three standard financial statements that are GAAP compliant. GAAP stands for Generally Accepted Accounting Principles. You might hear that acronym, so it helps to know what it means — which is that the business is following an approved, standardized format and formula for measuring, managing, and reporting the financials. Standards are good.

First, there's the income statement, which describes how much was sold, the costs of what was sold, and how much profit was made or how much money was lost. This is also more widely known as the P&L, which, as you have already learned if you didn't skip ahead, stands for the profit and loss statement. It really is the standard for measuring how profitable or not a business was (or will be) over a period of time, typically monthly, quarterly, and annually. Keep in mind that, within a company, there can also be numerous P&Ls as each product line, service, or division can have their own, according to how the business separates and/or combines itself. For example, there can be one P&L that includes everything in a kid's combo meal, i.e. the burger, fries, drink and toy, and treats it as one item using one P&L. Likewise, there can also be separate P&Ls for measuring the individual hamburgers, fries, drinks, and sundries.

The four basic elements of the P&L are:

- Gross Sales: Which represents sales from all sources.

- Gross Profit: Which deducts costs from gross sales.

- Expenses: Operating, selling, and administrative (SGA).

- Net Profit: Which subtracts expenses from gross profit.

Some businesspeople like to read the P&L from top to bottom, in other words, revenue first, then cost, then profit. Other people, including myself, prefer to read it from bottom to top, as profits and the cash it generates always matter more than revenue.

In their entirety, the P&L represents the business's overall sales, expenses, and earnings over a period of time. While it's used as a separate, standalone tool to help manage, measure, drive, anticipate, and adjust specific business within the company — it also ties into the company's general ledger. The general ledger ties together the financial records, which in turn, is used for the balance sheet.

The balance sheet is a "snapshot" of the company's overall financial standing at the present time, or in a specific moment in, and of time. It documents and profiles what the company owns (which are its assets) and what it owes (which are its liabilities). At the beginning, middle, and end of the day, the balance sheet should always balance with regard to assets equaling their liabilities' worth. Make sense?

The three basic elements of the balance sheet are:

- Assets: What the business owns and its net worth, including assets that can be liquidated, like cash, accounts receivables, and inventory; and long-term or fixed assets, like equipment and real estate; plus other assets, like intellectual property.

- Liabilities: What the business owes.

- Equity or Net Worth: Often called the "book value" of the company, it's basically the difference between assets and liabilities. In addition to book value, we also have what's called "goodwill," which includes the other assets of a company, like its brand, reputation, and market share. Goodwill is used to determine additional value and price for the company.

The third financial statement is much more important to home-based, small and midsize companies — most of which don't have the same size bank account and credit as the big guys. It's called the cash flow statement. For all intents and purposes, the cash flow statement is the best and most appropriate measurement of a company's day-to-day ability to pay their bills, make payroll, and basically stay open for business. Cash flow statements also help in:

- Anticipating problems.

- Uncovering obstacles and issues.

- Deliberating about investments.

- Determining a change in direction.

- Other business activity that depends on the companies' ability to take in cash, manage cash or spend cash.

Cash flow — and credit, to a lesser degree — are a company's lifeline, just like it is with your own personal bank account and credit cards. Imagine that, after an expensive, fun-filled weekend, you find yourself with only fifty bucks in your checking account on Monday, and you don't get paid until Friday. Has that ever happened to you? Well, it's going to be hard to pay the cash-required bills that are due that week, let alone feed yourself or go out for a night on the town, unless you're willing and ready to bounce some checks, use a high-interest credit card (if you can), or one of those rip-off cash-forwarding services. Clearly, that's not the way to do it. So mind your cash flow and mind your credit. Credit is good (if you can pay it off), but cash is king, in business and in life.

This also goes to prove the main point that profitable revenue; the cash that it generates, and the credit that it can establish — is the most important aspect of any company. You can always have revenue, but revenue doesn't pay the bills like payroll, rent, and such. Only cash pays the bills. If you make enough cash and can save it, that can also help pay the bills in the future. Or you can reinvest some back into the business for purposes of growth and expansion. Or you can give raises, and pay out cash as dividends and bonuses. That's why we like cash, most of all. Better yet, we like after-tax net cash, the cash that you get to keep (versus that

EBITDA stuff), because that's the truest justification for getting paid, getting raises, getting dividends and bonuses, and the value of the business or company. Raises, dividends and bonuses are good.

This also validates another point, in that good and accurate information and communication is invaluable; not just information that pertains to the numbers and the economics, but to everything. When conducting business, especially when we are in meetings, sending e-mails, or other types of written correspondence — we typically don't have a lot of time for a lot of words, wavering thoughts, rambling sentences, and idle chatter. Yeah, I know what you're thinking: something about that being ironic coming from me; but this is a book after all, so it gives me permission to be more "talkative." But seriously, in business, we like to keep things very focused — short and simple, but not simplistic. We say what we mean, and we mean what we say. With precision and timeliness.

When writing or talking to someone on a business level and discussing business objectives, we should always keep in the front of our mind two words whenever contemplating content, direction, scope, and overall purpose of our communication. Those two words are: "So what?" In other words, before we write what we write and say what we say, we need to ask ourselves, "What am I trying to do? What am I trying to say? What's my goal? What's the expected or desired outcome, action, or result?" If we can't answer the "so-what" question — then keep working on it, or move on, or forget about it. Depending on the situation, sometimes less is more. Sometimes more is more. And sometimes it's best to stay quiet.

To sum up, good companies need viable and valued products, and/or services, and/or solutions. They also need good operations, systems, the infrastructure, and the technology to help market, sell, fulfill, measure, stay informed, and support their products, services and solutions. Most importantly, they need good people to get everything done.

And always remember, although revenue's important, as that's ultimately how we get to profits, profits matter more — especially after-tax profits, the cash it generates, and how it's used to enhance the company's value, grow the business, make payroll, and give raises, dividends and bonuses.

KNOW YOUR COMPANY (and the company you keep)

According to the author William Ward, who's truly got some fantastic quotes, there are four steps to achievement:

1. To plan purposefully

2. Prepare prayerfully

3. Proceed positively

4. Pursue persistently

I think these steps correlate well with how you should start your new job, whether you're already onboard or just getting ready. You see, the better you know your company and your specific *to-dos*, the better you'll perform. The better you perform, the more you can help your colleagues, and (quickly) contribute and excel.

Speaking of jobs ... they're not always easy to get, especially those that you might want and have training in. You might have to take a job you don't want just to get your foot in the door. Most importantly, earn a paycheck. As it pertains to work, sometimes we have to do what we have to do. I think it's neat how Martin Luther King put it, "If a man is called to be a street sweeper, he should sweep streets even as Michelangelo painted, or Beethoven composed music, or Shakespeare wrote poetry. He should sweep streets so well that all the hosts of heaven and Earth will pause to say, 'Here lived a great street sweeper who did his job well.'" I'd also add that, just because we start as a street sweeper, it doesn't mean that we'll always be one, especially if our PAAM and work ethic are as Dr. King suggested.

There are countless examples of this, where young people have not only accepted jobs that they didn't really want, but did them with passion, energy, and desire. More importantly, they performed exceptionally well, delivering quick results in an expedient fashion. Heck, if I can do it, so can you.

You see, after graduating from college in Chicago, the best job I could get was as a telemarketer, making about eighty calls a day. That wasn't the dream. Fast forward a few months later, dejected and downtrodden, I saw an infomercial after Letterman from mega-motivator, Tony Robbins. I bought the tapes, which set me back a couple hundred bucks that I couldn't afford. You know what, though? It worked. I listened to what he had to say, applying not just his techniques, but more importantly, his spirit for life — his PAAM. Within months of finishing the program, and after making a renewed commitment to myself and the job, I produced big sales in short-order. As a result, I was promoted and transferred to lead outside sales in a new branch office.

Please understand that I'm not telling you that to be a show-off, or to "toot my own horn," although sometimes in life, you have to humbly toot your own horn, especially if others won't toot it for you. This strategy is best used when interviewing for a job, seeking a promotion, or asking for a raise. This is incorrectly used on your first date, or if you can't live up to the music, and you get busted for wrongful tooting. Wrongful tooting is bad.

I know from personal experience and from witnessing others that, if we have the right PAAM, we can overcome most any obstacle. Granted, it takes plenty of work, stick-to-itiveness, and perseverance. President Calvin Coolidge said, "Nothing in the world can take the place of perseverance. Talent will not; nothing is more common than unsuccessful individuals with talent. Genius will not; unrewarded genius is almost a proverb; Education will not; the world is full of educated derelicts. Persistence and determination alone are omnipotent." Persistence and determination are good.

So again, as far as your new job goes, you need to take the time to study the company and anything that pertains to the company, as it's very impressive to see a well-prepared interviewee or new employee. After all, you never get a second chance to make a good first impression, so make it a great one. Better yet, make it a series of great ones, as you will most certainly be meeting, seeing, and working with lots of new people. These people, in turn, may talk about you to other people, and in turn, other people. People talk.

This brings me to the second use of the word "company," and that's the company you keep within the company. Specifically, it's the people you befriend and associate with inside and outside of work. Which brings me back to the aforementioned "creeping-meatball" theory. Company meatballs — and no, I'm not talking about what we put into spaghetti, stuff in a bun, or eat from a stick — are the types of people who act like those meatballs: you know, sitting around, soaking up the sauce, and basically doing nothing. Meatballs are slackers; folks with bad attitudes who do less than their fair share, but bitch and moan about the workload nevertheless. Meatballs talk too much and work too little. They tend to badmouth the performers that get things done. More often than not, meatballs like to bellyache about the company's issues (all companies have issues), whether they're real or imaginary. Company meatballs are bad, as opposed to barbecued meatballs, which are good. Here are some differences between performers and meatballs.

- Performers work hard, work smart, and get things done. Meatballs just go through the motions.

- Performers are players who like teamwork and know how to block, tackle, defend, and score. Meatballs are selfish spectators who just sit, complain, and can only keep the score.

- Performers win, lose, and take risks. Meatballs do neither.

- Performer talk about "we" and "us" and "our." Meatballs talk about "they" and "them."

- Performers get it done and make it happen. Meatballs get in the way and watch it happen.

- Performers do it in real time, all the time. Meatballs need replays, and do-over's.

- Performers have genuine pride and are paid to perform. Meatballs just want to get paid.

Meatballs are also always looking to recruit others to be in their meatball gang, especially young and vulnerable new employees who may not know any better. If you're not careful, you'll find yourself directly or indirectly associated with them. Worst of all, you could find yourself joining them. That's how we get creeping meatballism. So be careful of the meatballs. The best defense against this is a good offense. A good offense means being a performer who performs and is known for performing. So be a performer, or for reasons I'll never understand, be a meatball. But please, on behalf of everyone, don't ever be a meatball disguised as a performer. That's just wrong.

That's enough about meatballs. For one, it's making me hungry. Two, it doesn't deserve any more time. What does deserve more time and appreciation is one of the most important elements in business, and it's summed up in one word: Expectations.

One of the best things that we can do to ensure short-term and long-term satisfaction, achievable results, and success — as opposed to frustration and failure — is to set realistic expectations. While we appreciate the fact that people are critical and make the ultimate difference, and that a company needs good products and good customer service, as well as the operations, systems, and technology infrastructure to market, sell and support themselves — we can't get where we want to go comfortably, without setting realistic expectations. And these expectations need to be rationalized and supported by good reasoning and explainable economics.

Nike's "Just Do It" mentality is cool for working out, but that maxim will get us into trouble in business. Everything we do should be planned and have understandable expectations, especially what we control. Unfortunately, while most of us would agree that expectations need to be realistic, you'll find some businesspeople, and some parents for that matter, who don't share that same view.

Due to the constant pressures that every company has to sell more, save more, do more, and make more — some people inappropriately set unrealistic expectations. They might sound bold and adventurous on the front end, but they'll get them into trouble on the back end, when they're unable to meet, let alone exceed, those expectations.

I'd also like to make a distinction between expectations and goals. There is a difference, as goals should be a subset to expectations. For example, it's all right to set "stretch-goals," which, in theory, are typically goals that go above and beyond the primary expectation. If you hit the stretch-goals, great! If you don't, you at least should have met the original expectation. You'll hear a lot about stretch-goals in business. Likewise, you'll hear a lot about exceeding expectations.

While all of us should be fans of exceeding expectations (as long as they're based on actual reality), we need to watch out if our job or the business we're in is set-up for constantly making its stretch-goals and exceeding expectations. If that's an expectation, it's a bad one. Try to avoid that. If you always work from and are measured on bad expectations, it's going to be difficult and painful. Over time, it's going to cause frustration. Frustration is bad.

Let's bring back the CEO of YourCo, so that she can frame her expectations. This should give you a feel for what a company might expect from a high-level, broad-strokes expectations standpoint:

Each of us sets demanding, yet realistic, expectations and a comprehensive portfolio of goals that, when achieved, make the person, our organization, and the entire company a winner. In addition, we expect each and every one of us to say what we mean and do what we say. We will meet or exceed realistic expectations with courtesy, respect, and appreciation. It is our responsibility to communicate concisely and precisely what's going on with simplicity and clarity. We will be known for doing what we say we'll do, on time, with a smile and good cheer. We'll work fast, but we won't hurry. When we hurry, mistakes happen. Our clients will like us for what we do, how we do it, and who we are. We work with and for our clients. We're a team.

We also know that continuous improvement is critical. Everything in our business, including us personally, can be improved and should get better every day. We hire, mentor, and support the best people, and we make it worth their while to stay with the company. We're humble. We have fun, and we enjoy balance between our commitments at work, at home, and in life.

In summary:

- *We expect everyone to understand our priorities*

  1) *Keep Momentum: Stay focused, deliver, and don't mess up what's working*

  2) *Drive Progress: Fix what's not working and help us generate new growth*

- *We expect to meet or exceed individual and collective goals and objectives*

- *We expect uncompromising teamwork, empathy, and support*

- *We expect functional excellence and a commitment to accountability*

- *We expect everyone to do their jobs, and do their best to be the best at them*

- *We expect leadership, innovation, trust, integrity, humor, kindness, and fun*

- *We expect to achieve continuous growth and exceptional client service*

- *We expect everyone to say what they mean and do what they say*

- *We expect to celebrate good things; resolve the bad; and know the difference*

- *We expect to design, develop, and deliver trusted, reliable, high-quality products*

- *We expect to work fast, but not to hurry*

- *We expect to deliver profitable revenue, now and forever*

There you have it: our CEO's expectations framework. It stands to reason that the leaders of your company will share many of the same views and expectations as her. If you can understand and live up to most of those, you're good to go.

Let's close this section on another important topic, and that's leadership. Good leadership is good.

Notice the use of the word *good* versus more dynamic adverbs like *extraordinary*, *fantastic*, *brilliant*, or *incredible*. Undoubtedly, you've already noticed the extensive usage of the word *good* (and *bad*) throughout the book already. The reason is simple: while there may be lots of adjectives that have more impact and panache than *good* … *good* is still good (and *bad* is still bad).

When it comes to good leadership, good is great.

Sadly, good leadership is in short supply. It's a big problem for business. As such, it's impacting our society, economy, and the country in general. You see, good leaders aren't just the folks who run and manage organizations. Good leaders can also be the folks who sweep the company floors. Good leaders aren't always the smartest people or the best performers. Leaders and leadership is not something that's anointed or bought; given because of someone's title or their place in a hierarchical organization chart. Good leaders and good leadership are earned. It's not entitled or bequeathed. That said, we need everyone to do a better job at trying to be good leaders, and to a degree, to do a better job of being good followers … with a willingness to do <u>all</u> of the jobs.

If you want a startling insight into the magnitude of this problem, specifically that as a nation we might be falling behind some other countries like India and China with regard to our work ethic and work mentality, you're encouraged to read an extremely compelling book by Thomas Friedman called *The World is Flat*. It's an astonishing, eye-opening wake-up call for our country to get our act together with regard to our individual and collective attitude and responsibilities about labor, as well as the importance of us not just being good leaders, or just innovative and smart. It also tells us we need to be diligent workers who are willing and able to roll-up our sleeves and do what it takes to keep the jobs. If we're not careful and if we don't figure out how to better manage and compete with what's happening in regard to globalization and offshoring, we could be in a really sticky situation. The fact of the matter is, we're in one now.

As you probably know, offshoring is when companies send their work to foreign countries for cheaper labor. We're not just talking about manufacturing jobs and programming, but professions like web-design, engineering, management, research and development, accounting, drug discovery, legal, etc... At the risk of sounding like an alarmist, if we're not vigilant, we could find ourselves in an even bigger predicament, especially if we don't accept this reality, and deal with it, deal from it, and co-exist. I'm a fan of "right-shoring," which is a best-of-both strategy.

Excuse my tangent here, but couple this offshoring movement with our expensive, messed-up healthcare system and the certainty of global warming (if you haven't seen the movie *An Inconvenient Truth*, please do so, but without letting politics get in the way), we now have some potential trouble brewing: for us, our companies, and the industry of America. In the laws of trickle-down economics, we could see trouble for our economy, our country, and therefore, present generations and those generations after us. If you haven't read Friedman's book, please read it. If you haven't seen the movie, or read-up on the issues with regard to our environment (that includes both sides), please do so. If you don't do either, consider yourself warned. After all, warned is good. Indifference is bad.

I have a colleague and friend whose dealing firsthand with this offshoring reality in the heartland of America. He's running a project with a Japanese company that has a manufacturing plant in northern Kentucky. They recently bought some new enterprise-resource-planning software, or ERP, and needed to install it quickly and cheaply. ERP, or enterprise software, is the catch-all name for the software that helps to manage, drive, run, and measure companies. It can be very complex and cumbersome. It can include everything from manufacturing, distribution, and production, to human resources, sales, marketing, and finance. It can also be very costly, as the software itself is typically not cheap, and the work it takes to implement the solution is, more often than not, even more expensive.

In order to keep costs low, companies are having to offshore this work to foreign firms in foreign countries, because many of the U.S.-based outfits are just too expensive. In this case however, the other shore came to the States. Due to the type of work required, they've flown in four very talented, experienced, college educated programmers from India, who collectively live in a dingy, cheap, two-bedroom hotel, cook on hot plates, eat and drink from paper plates, and do laundry in the sink. They work fourteen-hour days, and make minimum wage in accordance to U.S. standards. Their busting their butts and making next to nothing doing it. But if you asked them, however, they would tell you that it's great, and that they're having fun, learning lots, and digging America. They'd also tell you that they're thankful for their jobs, but most of all, that they're making money, even though they miss their families, and are living in those conditions for an indefinite period of time.

Are you willing to do that? Are you willing to fly thirty-two hours every other week, live in a crummy hotel, eat foreign food, work fourteen-hour days, and miss your family and friends and your stuff, for pay you think is inferior to your standards?

Tangent over. Let's get back to talking about leadership.

So, here's a truckload of the key leadership qualities, attributes, and characteristics that make for a good leader. For that matter, these qualities make for good employees, good colleagues, good friends, and good people. Just remember, while it's simple and easy to read about these in a book, it's a whole other thing to actually internalize them, embrace them, use them, and more important, be them. Learning to be a good leader is a lifelong journey, a journey that will never end. But you have to start somewhere and do something, no matter who you are or where you come from. An embodiment of this determination is Elihu Burritt, a poor, "learned blacksmith," born in America in 1810. He was known for his self-improvement, writing, and pacifism. He became a highly regarded social reformist respected by prominent leaders, both in the United States and Europe. With regard to his life, Elihu wrote, "All that I have accomplished has been by the plodding, patient, persevering process of accretion, which build the ant heap particle by particle, thought by thought, fact by fact."

If a poor blacksmith in the 1800s, without the education, tools, and support that you have today, could become a renowned leader by intestinal fortitude, gutsy perseverance, and noble determination, well then, you can as well, can't you? Particle by particle. Thought by thought. Fact by fact.

GOOD LEADERS HAVE GOOD LEADERSHIP ...

Good leaders have integrity. They are ethical, humble, compassionate, and trustworthy.

Good leaders are stractical. They're good with both strategy and being tactical.

Good leaders set realistic, fact-based, and achievable expectations, goals, and objectives.

Good leaders execute. They get things done on time and on budget.

Good leaders comprehend the economics. They do the math and know how to measure.

Good leaders are productive, and they like productivity, efficiency, effectiveness, and quality.

Good leaders are good collaborators and communicators. They're understandable.

Good leaders achieve quick, short-term wins.

Good leaders are energetic and motivated. They work hard and have fun with it.

Good leaders are team players. They are empathetic, likable, and others-oriented.

Good leaders anticipate, adapt, and adopt. They're flexible.

Good leaders are accountable. They are organized and coordinated. They deliver.

Good leaders think outside and inside "the box." They get momentum and progress.

Good leaders are knowledgeable. They have real skills and broad perspectives.

Good leaders have conviction and are committed. They work hard and smart.

Good leaders keep things simple, not simplistic — and they know the difference.

Good leaders have a cause. It's about more than just making money.

Good leaders are authentic. They have humble confidence and positive pragmatism.

Good leaders do the hard and soft stuff. They can manage the books and the feelings.

Good leaders listen intently. They hear what people say and what they mean.

Good leaders rally for good change. They justify, promote, manage, and deliver change.

Good leaders are comfortable with ambiguity and uncertainty. They also like details.

Good leaders handle the pressure. They're thick-skinned and cool under duress.

Good leaders have solid memories. They remember and forget appropriately.

Good leaders are self-critical. They know that they make mistakes and can improve.

Good leaders reprimand in private and praise in public.

Good leaders know when enough is enough. They put first things first.

Good leaders are coaches. They want and nurture more good leaders.

Good leaders appreciate and promote a balanced life with regard to work and family. They get it.

Good leaders are also diplomatic, persistent and persevering, agreeable, unassuming, calm, polite, good-humored, exciting and excited, helpful, thoughtful, competitive, steady, brave, self-starting, conscientious, earnest, flexible, resolute, tolerant, spirited, cheerful, inclusive, congenial, patient, responsive, trusting, optimistic, loyal, and consistent. (Note: nothing frustrates employees more than convenient, inconsistent, disingenuous, in-title-only leaders.)

Now I know you're thinking: "Gee, Scott, that's a lot." Indeed it is. It just goes to show you that it's not easy, or probably even possible, for that matter, to have all of those qualities and characteristics. But here's the great news: you don't have to. For what it's worth, nobody has all of those attributes. Even if they have most of them, they always need more work and can always improve, and they'll be the first to admit it. Take it one day at a time. Be mindful of what makes up a good leader, and start to work at it: particle by particle, thought by thought, and fact by fact. If you do want to learn more about business leadership, you should at least read two books: *The Leadership Challenge*, by Kouzes and Posner, and *True North*, by Bill George with Peter Sims. Good stuff.

There's an old parable about a man walking down the street who happened to see a bricklayer laying bricks. Curious as to what was being built, the man walked up and asked the bricklayer what he was doing? The brick layer gruffly replied, "What's it look like I'm doing? I'm laying bricks." At that, the man walked around the corner and saw another bricklayer, who was laying bricks, as well. He decided to ask this man the same question. This worker happily and proudly replied, "I'm building a cathedral."

So, are you building a cathedral, or just laying bricks?

To sum up and to simplify the key elements of any good business, just remember my *5P* formula:

1) PEOPLE: Once again and for always, people are the most important assets of any organization, regardless of its size, industry, or location. Whether it's public or private, for profit or not, or even highly automated and technology driven, it makes no difference when it comes to the importance of people — especially good and talented people who are team-oriented, hard-working, reliable, nice, and have proper values and the right PAAM. Good people are good.

2) PRODUCT: It certainly helps to have a good product (which can also be a service and/or a solution) that people and other companies need, and want, to buy. And hopefully buy a lot of it. Keep in mind that companies and people buy stuff because they think it has value, and that it can and will do something for them in such a way that it motivates them to purchase it at a price that they can rationalize, from both a quantitative standpoint (price, affordability, ROI, etc.); and from a qualitative standpoint, in that it makes them feel better emotionally, physically, spiritually, etc.. Good products are good.

3) PROCESS: This is also referred to as operations, logistics, and supply-chain management (remember ERP?). This is how and what a business does tactically and systematically to perform, manage, and measure. In effect, this is how it executes and

gets things done. Companies need to be as efficient, effective, and productive as they can be, so the differences between good processes and bad processes can be significant, impacting not only customer service, sales, and profit … but teamwork, attitude, and morale. Good process is good.

4) PLANNING: This is where we do the work with regard to vision and strategy, but also with regard to improving the here-and-now. Companies, like people, must always be planning for change and progress. That includes planning for how to enhance the present and deal with the future in regard to competition, unforeseen problems, disruptions from new technology and products, employee attrition, changes in socio-economic policy, you name it. No business can exist long-term if they don't properly plan, change, anticipate, and improve. Good planning is good.

5) PROFIT: Business is in business to generate profitable revenue, so that it can pay for its people, products, processes, and planning —in other words, so it can exist. Only by existing can it have jobs with paychecks. Be responsible. Generate value. Pay taxes. Donate to charities that will help the community that the business and employees live in. Build new products, services, or solutions. Hire more people. Give raises, dividends and bonuses. And grow. While many businesses start without profit and/or use debt, that's only acceptable if the expectation is to repay those debts. You can only do that through the cash that comes from profit. Revenue is good. Profit is great. Cash is king. We can't pay for the porch lights and keep them on, without business and the cash it generates.

Business is good — especially good business.

LOVE, LEARN, WORK, AND ENJOY LIFE

Time to be Genuinely Exceptional

"We may affirm absolutely that nothing great in the world has been accomplished without passion."

GEORG HEGEL

I n the spirit of sharing and caring, allow me to express some final thoughts and recommendations, with the sincere hope that these closing comments, along with the other ideas and suggestions, will make a positive influence on you. More than that, my ultimate wish is that, in one small way or another, this book can help you succeed a little faster and a little easier both in business and in life. If it does, all I ask is for you to "pay it forward" down the road. When you're ready, and certain that the time is right, take the initiative and be a good mentor yourself. You don't have to write a book; just be a good coach. When you're ready, offer guidance and support to someone who can use your help. Help is good. Being helpful is even better.

I keep two Father's Day cards at my desk: one from my parents, and one from my wife. On the cover of the card from my parents is a picture of a young boy dressed in goggles, wearing one of those old-fashioned pilot's caps with the flaps that hang down over the ears.

He's standing on a box, with a towel wrapped around him like a cape. His arms are stretched out wide as if he is flying. He has a big smile and a marvelous look of pure enjoyment. The writing with the picture says, "*Son, from playing the hero...*" Then when you open the card, there's another picture of a grown man, walking on the beach with his child sitting on his shoulders, holding onto Dad's hands. They're playing happily in the waves. The caption underneath this picture, and in an obvious continuation of the sentiment from the cover reads, "*...To being the Hero.*" Then on the other side of the card is written: "*How wonderful it has been to watch you grow into the amazing man you are. Happy Father's Day.*" Then it's signed simply, "*Love You, Mom and Dad.*"

Now inside the card from my wife is a picture of our two children, happy as all get-out. Opposite of the picture are the following words: "'*Walk a little slower, Daddy,' said a child so small. 'I'm following in your footsteps and I don't want to fall. Sometimes your steps are very fast. Sometimes they're hard to see; so walk a little slower, Daddy, for you are leading me. Someday when I'm all grown up, you're what I want to be. Then I will have a little child who'll want to follow me. And I would want to lead just right, and know that I was true. So walk a little slower, Daddy, for I must follow you.*'"

I have to tell you, about a week or so after getting those cards, I brought them into my office and read them again, maybe ten times or more. They made me cry — and I'm not just talking about getting watery eyed. That happens even when I watch sappy TV. I'm talking about a caught-off-guard, grimacing, tears-rolling-down-my-face-crying-like-a-little-kid-kind-of-cry. Talk about a Hallmark moment.

In hindsight, I don't really know why the cards affected me like they did. Maybe I was having a bad day at the office, or had been short-tempered with my kids or my wife earlier that morning, and it made me remorseful. Or maybe it was because I really didn't think that I was worth such neat cards. Regardless, they did something besides generate tears. They still do.

The cards make me stop and reflect. They motivate me and make me appreciative of all that life has to offer, as well as the responsibilities and obligations that we have in life. The cards also impress upon me the fact that we have to be mindful of everything; that everything matters, and even what doesn't matter — matters.

You see, if it matters to you, but not to somebody else, it certainly matters, right? Intuitively then, if it matters to somebody else, but not to you, it still matters, though, because it matters to that person. That's why the so-called "Golden Rule" is flawed. It shouldn't be, "Treat people the way *you* want to be treated." After all, "you" could be a real jerk and think it's okay to treat, and be treated, like a jerk. What the Golden Rule actually should say is, "Treat people the way *they* want to be treated." That's assuming they're not devil-worshipping, sadomasochists into bad music. That is not good.

But seriously, it's not just a difference in wordsmithing — it's not. There's a fundamental differentiation in the philosophy between the two interpretations. Simply stated, one's *self-oriented* and one's *others-oriented*. Because you're savvy, you'll agree. As importantly, you'll appreciate the difference and choose the right one. After all, you're cool enough to read this book, willing enough to get this far, and smart enough to hang in there until the end. That says something about your ability to learn, to be challenged, and to accept different interpretations and points of view. That said, there will be those who disagree with us (assuming we think alike) and pundits who will say that we're wrong, or at a minimum, overly sensitive, and just not tough enough. That's okay. They can, and should, have their own opinions. After all, opinions are like belly buttons: we all have them. How you manage them however, is what it's all about. The writer F. Scott Fitzgerald said, "the ability to hold two opposing ideas in mind at the same time and still retain the ability to function" is the sign of a truly intelligent person. And you can do that, can't you?

Again and as always, everything matters. Most of all ...

That we're compassionate. There's a terrific book by Harry Palmer called, *Resurfacing: Techniques for Exploring Consciousness*, that recommends a five step-exercise for putting compassion in action. It goes like this: With your attention focused on the other person, be it a friend or stranger, tell yourself, that:

- Step 1: "Just like me, this person is seeking happiness in his/her life."

- Step 2: "Just like me, this person is trying to avoid suffering in his/her life."

- Step 3: "Just like me, this person has known sadness, loneliness and despair."

- Step 4: "Just like me, this person is seeking to fill his/her needs."

- Step 5: "Just like me, this person is learning about life."

It matters that we go to work and that we do our best work. But it also matters that we do so smartly and in recognition of why we work, which is to provide for and secure that which is important.

It matters that there is too much violence, hatred, injustice, pain, and suffering. We need to do what we can, in our own way, to help the discriminated against, the sick, and the less fortunate.

It matters that we have values and ethics, that we can be trusted and trust, that we genuinely listen and genuinely learn, and that we're empathetic and sensitive.

It matters that we can be individuals with individuality, but that we can also be sensitive, others-oriented, and mindful of what others think, feel, and what they're going through.

It matters that we are disciplined and accountable, that we do what we say and say what we'll do, and that we can take and accept criticism and respond accordingly.

It matters that we can promote, embrace, manage, and deliver change; that we are both realistic and idealistic; and that we know the difference between when, where, and why.

It matters that we can disagree agreeably and that we can take the high-road and turn the other cheek.

It matters that we keep tabs on our finances and manage our cash flow and credit; that we only spend what we can, and only buy what we should. Debt stinks.

It matters that we care for our environment and deal with the "inconvenient truth" of global warming; that we respect our world and do our part to keep it clean and healthy.

It matters that we're always improving ourselves — our minds, bodies, values, and spirit. It matters that we promote quality in work and life.

It matters that we love unconditionally and that we bestow love and receive love. It also matters that we parent conditionally and respect the job of parenting.

It matters that we appreciate our individual and collective responsibilities to ourselves, our families, and our friends — and yes, our companies, colleagues, country, and world.

It matters that we laugh, listen to music, sing, dance, stay fit, read, work, enjoy life, learn, and strive to be genuinely exceptional.

* (This space has been left blank for your own unique "matters." Talk about it with family and friends. Think big.)

On that note, let's end the book just as it started: by thanking you.

Thanks for your time, mind, heart, body, and spirit. While I can't express my gratitude in person and give you a friendly hug, I want you to know that your commitment to being the very best that you can be, and having the right PAAM will mean a lot to the company you work for, as well as the company you keep.

Your success is significant to your friends, our country, and whether you can see it or believe it, our planet. Most importantly of all, your success means so very much on the behalf of family, yours and others'. That includes grandparents and parents, as well as yours and other people's children.

So while good first impressions are important, it's never too late to start making good lasting impressions that mean something now and after we're gone. What should people say about you today? What do you want them to say about you today? And how do you want to be known, tomorrow and beyond?

The Swami Sivananda said, "Put your heart, mind, intellect, and soul even into your smallest acts. This is the secret to success." And to quote William Ward again, "Do more than belong: participate. Do more than care: help. Do more than believe: practice. Do more than be fair: be kind. Do more than forgive: forget. Do more than dream: work."

And that my friend, is what it's all about …

What you put into you …

How you manage and develop you …

To help make you and us the best that we can be …

So that we can accelerate our mutual success …

Enjoy good careers and good livelihoods …

And live happy, loving, compassionate, family-oriented …

Time of our life lives.

That's all good.

Thanks again. Peace and joy to you and the world.

Take care.

SCOTT ABBOTT is an authentic leader. He's an innovator, entrepreneur, and philanthropist. He has started companies, managed companies, and worked with hundreds of organizations, and thousands of people from around the world. He is a student and teacher of business and life. However, he thinks of himself foremost as a son, husband, father, friend and humanist. It was in this spirit of familial passion, caring, and commitment - coupled with what he calls his "heartfelt civic duty" - that he wrote Pocket PorchLights. When Scott's not working, speaking, or coaching ... he's enjoying life with his family and friends. You can visit Scott at www.pocketporchlights.com, or email him at scott@pocketporchlights.com.